PELICAN BOOKS

MIND THE STOP

G. V. Carey's working life, after taking an honours degree in classics (and getting a Rugby Blue) at Cambridge, was divided between schoolmastering and publishing, with interruptions for service in two World Wars, in the Rifle Brigade and the R.A.F. respectively. He was Educational Secretary of the Cambridge University Press from 1922 to 1929, and Headmaster of Eastbourne College from 1929 until 1938.

Besides writing *Mind the Stop*, G. V. Carey compiled the official Cambridge University War List after the 1914–18 war, and was part-author of an outline history of that war. Other works include *Making an Index* (1951), *American into English* (1953) and *Punctuation* (1957).

G. V. CAREY

MIND
THE STOP

*A Brief Guide to
Punctuation
with a Note on
Proof-Correction*

PENGUIN BOOKS

Penguin Books Ltd, Harmondsworth, Middlesex, England
Penguin Books Inc., 7110 Ambassador Road, Baltimore, Maryland 21207, U.S.A.
Penguin Books Australia Ltd, Ringwood, Victoria, Australia

—

First published by the Cambridge University Press 1939
Revised edition published 1958
Published in Pelican Books 1971

—

Copyright © Cambridge University Press, 1958

—

Made and printed in Great Britain by
Cox & Wyman Ltd,
London, Reading and Fakenham
Set in Monotype Bembo

To
STANLEY MORISON
whose encouragement
(however much he may now regret it)
first inspired me to try my hand
at this task

CONTENTS

PREFACE

IN writing this book I have had more especially in mind three classes of readers: those who, professionally or otherwise, are faced with the task of reading proofs; those who at school are learning to write English correctly (and perhaps a few of their teachers, *quorum pars parva fui*); and those ordinary folk – I have met plenty – who remark somewhat vaguely 'I know nothing about punctuation', and occasionally add, not very purposefully, 'Where can I find out something about it?' I can only hope that I have not, in consequence, fallen between three stools; and moreover that the name of the place (see below) at which my task has been carried out may not prove to have a sinister application. Anyhow this is far from being a 'high-brow' book and I have deliberately refrained from using more of the technical phraseology of grammar and syntax than has been absolutely necessary. At the same time I have assumed that such elementary terms as 'co-ordinate', 'subordinate', 'antecedent', 'relative clause' are unlikely to cause any difficulty to anybody.

Of the many examples that I have used by way of illustration a few have of necessity had to come out of my own head, but far more are taken from books and newspapers of recent date. I gladly take this opportunity of acknowledging my indebtedness to those numerous writers, mostly unknown, who have not given me permission to make use of their work.

Lastly, if I may be forgiven a spasm of self-consciousness, I wish to state that, even had it not so befallen that much of this book was written during a time of almost unexampled crisis, I should have been under no illusion about the importance of my subject. The mind of one who happens to have an eye for a comma is not necessarily incapable of comprehending larger issues or embracing wider interests.

BOREHAM STREET   G. V. C.
January 1939

PREFACE TO THE SECOND EDITION

YEARS of reading (and proof-correcting) since this book first appeared have served to confirm rather than to shake my views on the principles of punctuation, but they have in some respects affected their emphasis. I have therefore welcomed this opportunity of bringing the book up to date by the addition of a new chapter; by some rewriting throughout – chiefly in Chapters 3 (in The Comma section especially), 4, and 5; and by freely substituting more recent and sometimes, I hope, rather more apt illustrations.

Most of those who have any views at all on punctuation have strong ones, and I had been quite prepared to find some of mine, if vouchsafed any attention whatever, provoking contradiction or, at the least, controversy. Instead I have been most agreeably surprised by the amount of favour they have found with both reviewers and personal correspondents. I am sincerely grateful for the encouragement afforded by many writers from near and far – most of them strangers, one at least now become a valued friend – and have benefited from such suggestions as they have offered. My warmest debt of gratitude is due to an old friend and former colleague, Mr R. J. L. Kingsford, the present Secretary to the Syndics of the Press, for his unfailing helpfulness and consideration.

MIDHURST   G. V. C.
1958

BY WAY OF INTRODUCTION

To say that no two persons punctuate exactly alike would no doubt be an exaggeration, but most people would probably agree that punctuation is a matter not only of rules but of personal taste. I feel, therefore, that before getting down to details, which must necessarily involve some degree of laying down the law, I may be excused for stating some personal views on the general principles of punctuation. Readers who are anxious to 'cut the cackle' may prefer to skip this chapter, but if, having done so, they find themselves at loggerheads with me later on, they must remember that they have missed part of the plot.

I should define punctuation as being governed two-thirds by rule and one-third by personal taste. I shall endeavour not to stress the former to the exclusion of the latter, but I will not knuckle under to those who apparently claim for themselves complete freedom to do what they please in the matter. Apart from the professed cranks, there are the unmannerly style-hogs of the 'popular' press whose reckless Remingtons run riot over the page, leaving mutilated fragments of sentence writhing in their tracks. Here is an instance, taken at random from one of the Sunday illustrated papers:

Lady *X* refuses all blandishments to go on the stage or into films. Though her sister, Lady *Y*, is an actress. Appearing in 'People of Our Class'.

What is the point of this sort of thing? Is it meant to convey a subtle form of humour or merely to be snappy? I can see in it nothing but wilful murder of the mother tongue, scarcely more excusable than any other form of matricide. And, be it noted, the crime is committed solely by the punctuation; a perfectly normal sentence has been ruthlessly hacked into three bits, with the result that one bit still lives and the other two are cut off in their prime.

As for the professed cranks aforesaid, I use the term with no personal disrespect, for I have in mind one in particular who was both scholar and saint, and whose friendship I was proud to possess. He would punctuate thus, not absent-mindedly but on principle:

Bible-making was collecting selecting editing.

Actual events conversations characters form the theme through which strange harmonies develop.

Then Job 'takes up his own parable', opening with a lyric Hymn of Wisdom, in which he sings the mystery of God's transcendence in calmer strain part hopeful part resigned wholly yearning.

I fancy that most readers must find this sort of thing a little tiresome, and occasionally downright confusing. At the least it can fairly be described as cranky. Other writers also have peculiar methods of their own, but this book is concerned rather with common errors than with exceptional oddities.

Let it be granted that the punctuation, like the spelling, of the English language has been subject to change in the course of centuries – one has only to observe the punctuation of the Bible in order to become aware of this; yet there would seem to be no reason why the one should not become, at least to some extent, standardized by time and usage, as the other has been. In so far, then, as I shall lay down the law, I shall base it on the standards that I find in the best type of newspaper, such as *The Times*, modified occasionally by my own sense of what is fitting and reasonable.

It is as well to be agreed at the start on what is the purpose of punctuation. I fancy that there are some who feel that the main purpose of stops is to indicate the pauses or breathing-spaces appropriate in reading, with the possibility of reading aloud never quite lost sight of; at all events there are some styles of punctuation that would seem to imply such a view. And this of course *is* one of the functions of punctuation, especially of the full stops that separate sentence from sentence, and to some extent also of the minor stops within a sentence. But of all that is written and printed only a small fraction is read aloud, and it must be remembered that the needs of the eye are not exactly the same as those of the voice. The first essential is that the meaning of what is written should be conveyed to the reader's mind, through his eye, with the least possible delay and without any ambiguity. I would say, therefore, that the main function of punctuation is *to make perfectly clear the construction* of the written words. If this function is properly fulfilled, then automatically all risk of ambiguity will be avoided and the appropriate pauses will be indicated to the reader, when they are not so optional as to be left to him to supply.

These may seem to some to be the veriest truisms and to others to be vague generalizations. To the latter at any rate some illustration might be helpful at this stage. Here is a sentence with commas inserted at points where a slight pause might be made, or breath taken, if the words were spoken or read aloud:

The whole country and the British Commonwealth, followed the visit of the King and Queen to France last week, and that visit must have left on those who were privileged to accompany their Majesties, an impression that will not easily be forgotten.

The reader who promptly detects superfluous commas here is quite right, but he will find plenty of examples, if not always quite so obvious, of this *method* of punctuation in his every-day reading (see also pp. 44–5); and he may also be reminded that two centuries ago that sentence might well have been punctuated almost exactly as above. Modern usage has tended towards increasing economy in punctuation, and in fact *The Times* printed that sentence unbroken by any stop from start to finish. Nor, so far as the *construction* of the sentence is concerned, is any stop needed. The first comma is obviously wrong; it merely interposes an unnecessary break between the subject ('The whole country and the British Commonwealth') and its verb ('followed'). The same applies to the last comma, which makes an unnecessary break between the verb ('left') and its direct object ('an impression'); but here the needless intrusion of the comma is a little less obvious owing to the length of the clause and the fact that the indirect object ('on those who . . . Majesties') has been inserted before the direct object. One might in fact reckon that, if not more than 5 per cent of 'general writers' (to coin a term parallel to 'the general reader') would have put a comma after 'Commonwealth', something like 30 per cent might have put one after 'Majesties'; yet the principle which makes both inadmissible is precisely the same.

With the remaining comma, between 'week' and 'and', we are on different ground. Between two words or phrases joined by 'and' (e.g. 'The whole country and the British Commonwealth') a comma is obviously out of place. Similarly between two *clauses* joined by 'and' a comma is generally held to be unnecessary, at all events when such clauses are comparatively short – 'the rain ceased and the sun came out'; and especially when the subject is unchanged – 'the sun came out and soon dried the streets'. But it is possible for clauses (even with subject unchanged) to be of such length that a comma before the 'and' that joins them comes as an aid to the eye as well as marking a pause for the voice, and it might be argued that this applies to the sentence which we have been examining. (The observant reader will note that I have applied this consideration to the sentence which he has just read.) Here in fact is one of those cases in which personal taste must be the deciding factor, and the writer who prefers to make a slight break in the rather long sentence I have quoted by putting a comma after 'week' is perfectly justified in doing so.

The point which I am chiefly concerned to establish, however, is that, in the main, the insertion of stops should be governed more by the construction of the sentence than by its mere length. I stress this point because I believe that faulty punctuation is often due to the temptation to drop an occasional stop into a long sentence at points where it is felt that the speaking voice might momentarily pause for breath, without proper regard to the construction of the sentence; and that this temptation, though specially common with schoolboy (or schoolgirl) writers, is by no means confined to them.

This matter of punctuating in accordance with the construction, or syntax, of the sentence perhaps needs further illustration.

Counsel maintained that the accused if he had as was alleged by some though not the most reliable of the witnesses for the prosecution taken the articles in question had been subject to a temporary lapse of memory as a result of shell-shock sustained during the War.

Few will deny that this sentence, even if it presents no actual ambiguity as it stands, is rather involved (not to say clumsy), and that the grasp of its meaning will be made more immediate by some means of marking out its clauses. Moreover, it is the reader's eye that instinctively feels this need before any question of speaking the words arises.

We have here a main clause, 'Counsel maintained that the accused had been subject to a temporary lapse of memory as a result of shell-shock sustained during the War.' Subordinate to this is the clause 'if he had taken the articles in question'. This clause is itself qualified by the further clause 'as was alleged by some of the witnesses for the prosecution', into which again is inserted the further qualification of the word 'some' – 'though not the most reliable'. I myself find it helpful to employ, by a kind of half-conscious mental process, on such sentences the method of those old 'bracket' affairs in algebra that I used to enjoy unravelling – almost my only pleasant recollection of algebra, in fact.

Translating this for once in a way into black and white, we get the following:

Counsel maintained that the accused [if he had {as was alleged by some (though not the most reliable) of the witnesses for the prosecution} taken the articles in question] had been subject to . . . War.

Thus we have dissected the various clauses of which this sentence is composed; but it remains a sentence which must run on from start to finish without any major break and consequently calls nowhere for any heavier stop than a comma. We therefore replace each bracket by a comma and the sentence finally reads as follows:

Counsel maintained that the accused, if he had, as was alleged by some, though not the most reliable, of the witnesses for the prosecution, taken the articles in question, had been subject to a temporary lapse of memory as a result of shell-shock sustained during the War.

The result is a plentiful sprinkling of commas, but they are not sprinkled at random; they mark out the construction of the sentence, which, I submit, is not over-punctuated. Some might object that the commas marking off the phrase 'though not the most reliable' are fussy and might prefer to dispense with them; personally I find them helpful. Others indeed might choose to replace them by actual brackets, as a relief from the surrounding commas. But in any case the number of stops does not depend primarily on the *length* of the sentence. It would be easy to construct a sentence just as long, or longer, requiring no stop at all.

Counsel for the prosecution said that the evidence proved

beyond any possible doubt that on the morning in question the accused had wilfully and deliberately removed a number of articles displayed on the counter of the plaintiff's shop and that at the time of doing so he had been fully responsible for his actions.

This sentence (which in fact consists of fifty-four words, compared with forty-eight in the previous one) comprises just two straightforward clauses – 'on the morning ... plaintiff's shop', 'at the time ... his actions' – joined by 'and [that]' and put in the form of an indirect statement by the opening words 'Counsel ... doubt that'. The sentence is nowhere qualified by a subordinate clause of any sort and there is no obvious need of any break or stop in it anywhere. It is certainly a long sentence, and a comma between 'shop' and 'and that ...', separating the two main clauses, would not be objectionable, though the two clauses are so closely connected in sense as to make it unnecessary. Any kind of stop inserted at any other point would not really help the reader and would merely interrupt the run of the sentence.

In the much bracketed, and subsequently much comma'd, instance given above we were up against the 'clause-within-a-clause' problem. In the normal course of writing one is more often concerned with clauses or sentences that lie side by side, and then the problem lies in the degree of pause or break required between such clauses or sentences; in other words, we have to choose between the comma, the semi-colon (or occasionally the colon), and the full-stop.

In this connection I should like to make about the comma in particular one further point that seems to me to be important as a general principle and yet to be not always clearly recognized. A single comma makes a more pronounced break in a sentence than commas used in pairs. The latter are equivalent to what one might describe as a mild pair of brackets, and consequently while in one sense they do of course make a certain slight break, in another sense they serve to lighten the break between the words preceding and following them. Stated in general terms this may sound paradoxical, but I think that illustration will make the point quite clear. The sentence quoted on p.18 provides a handy example.

. . . As was alleged by some, though not the most reliable of the witnesses for the prosecution. . . .

The single comma after 'some' sets up a small barrier between that word and 'of the witnesses . . .', though the latter words belong closely to the former in sense. It has in fact this sort of effect:

As was alleged by some | though not the most reliable of the witnesses for the prosecution.

Incidentally this punctuation at once introduces a slight ambiguity, for the clause might now mean 'as was alleged by some *people* (not necessarily witnesses), though not by the most reliable of the *witnesses* . . .'. Instead of helping to make the construction (and consequently the meaning) clear, it confuses it. Therefore it is wrong, though it is the kind of mistake that is very commonly made. But put in another comma after 'reliable', and the effect is quite different.

. . . As was alleged by some, though not the most reliable, of the witnesses for the prosecution. . . .

The reader is bound to feel that the second comma, so far from making the separation between 'some' and 'of the witnesses' more marked, has helped to bring them nearer to each other in sense, because the *pair of commas* has very much the same effect as brackets – 'by some (though not the most reliable) of the witnesses ...'. Actual brackets, as I pointed out earlier, might quite suitably be used here; but, even if they were not felt to be too heavy or fussy in this particular context, their incessant use wherever a pair of commas would serve the same purpose would become extremely tiresome to the eye. Yet the job of both is essentially the same, and I believe that the failure to realize this as a fundamental principle, and the consequent failure to follow up a comma at the beginning of a subordinate clause by another one at the end of it, lead to more than half the mistakes of punctuation, often trivial but occasionally quite misleading.

If I were to say more by way of introduction I should soon find myself involved in matters which demand detailed treatment in their proper place. I will close these general remarks by summarizing my own view of the subject in a couple of sentences. Stops should be used as sparingly as sense will permit; but in so far as they are needed for an immediate grasp of the sense or for the avoidance of any possible ambiguity, or occasionally to relieve a very lengthy passage, they should be used as freely as need be. The best punctuation is that of which the reader is least conscious; for when punctuation, or the lack of it, obtrudes itself, it is usually because it offends.

2

THE HEAVIER STOPS

Full-Stop – Colon – Semi-Colon

WITH every desire to be methodical, I am going to find it difficult to subdivide my subject tidily and compactly; and though I should have liked to devote a short chapter to each kind of stop I can see that an attempt to proceed strictly on those lines will not work. If, for instance, one is concerned with the wrong use of a comma where a semi-colon or a full-stop would be right, under which heading is the matter to be dealt with? The nature of the subject is such that one thing *will* keep trespassing on another's ground, and I have tried to compromise by treating separately what I have called the 'heavier' and the 'lighter' stops. Even so there is bound to be a certain amount of overlapping or cross-reference, though I will try not to harass the reader with more of either than is absolutely necessary. In this matter I have endeavoured to make the index as helpful to him as possible.

THE FULL-STOP. – 'Every schoolboy knows' that full-stops come at the end of sentences; and seeing that a sentence has got to contain at least one main clause, with its own finite verb, quite apart from any subordinate clause that may be added, one would have thought that this was about all that need be said on the subject. But that would be reckoning without the 'popular' journalist of today and, as the daily picture-papers and suchlike in which he corrupts the language circulate, I suppose, amongst a larger public than any other form of reading-matter (I avoid the word 'literature' in this connection), I am afraid that he has got to be reckoned with. That, coupled with the desire to show that I have not just stumbled on a single 'freak' instance, is my only excuse for paying more attention to the kind of atrocity that I referred to at the foot of p. 13. In point of fact, anyone who glances at the effusions of the so-called 'gossip writers', for instance, will find this type of thing any day of the week:

Talking of golf, the Duke of X never uses a tee when driving. Just drops the ball and bangs it away.

If he uses a tee he is likely to fluff or make an air-shot. As he did with his inaugural drive as president of St Andrews.

Serious and detailed comment on this sort of stuff might seem superfluous, but I remind myself that this book may find its way into schools, where the needs of some of its readers may be rather elementary. So here goes.

The second 'sentence' possesses a finite verb, it is true – in fact two; but the omission of any subject to them, presumably meant to be playful, merely robs the sentence of any dignity it might have had. In any case this sentence is so closely connected in sense with its predecessor that a semi-colon would be preferable to a full-stop after 'driving'; but so long as the 'he' is omitted before 'just drops' you may put any stop you like, or none, at that point and you won't get an English sentence.

The last 'sentence' is in fact a subordinate clause depending closely on the main verb of the preceding clause, 'he is likely to . . .'. To put anything but a comma after 'air-shot' is pointless and tiresome, and will not pass muster even as a colloquialism.

Note in passing how utterly out of place is the new paragraph at 'If he uses . . .'. I shall have more to say on that subject later.

Here is another example, which calls for scarcely any comment:

I stayed at Ayr for the Exhibition. The guest of Colonel *Y* at *Blank*, his beautiful estate on the river.

It is enough to remark that the words 'The guest . . . river' do not even constitute a clause, for they contain no verb at all. They belong inseparably to 'I stayed' and nothing heavier than a comma after 'Exhibition' should separate them therefrom. If the word 'as' were inserted before 'the guest', even that comma could go.

Unhappily the trouble does not quite end there. Whether or not the infection is spreading from below, misuse of the full-stop seems to be getting more common and is to be found – in less blatant form, it is true – in better writers. Even *The Times* lately descended to:

Thus England were eight for two when May came in. Once more with the cares of the world on his shoulders.

And the following, by a very well-known writer, is quoted from a no less reputable journal:

It is not enough to respite the peace of this year by methods that would only intensify the discords and dangers of the future. Methods that would so deeply embitter the relations of Britain and Germany as to make their hostility once more incurable and lasting peace almost unthinkable; with no hope, meanwhile, of restoring any settled world's basis of happiness, confidence, and prosperity.

There is of course nothing in this so offensive as the kind of thing I have just been quoting; but why the full-stop after 'of the future'? It leaves the sentence immediately following without any main verb; in fact it is not a *sentence* at all. The whole passage 'Methods that would so deeply embitter ... and prosperity' is simply a *clause* expanding the preceding 'methods that would only intensify ... the future'. It belongs to that opening clause and cannot stand on its own feet as a separate sentence; yet the full-stop makes it try to do so. The whole extract, indeed, is a single indissoluble sentence – and a pretty long one too; but if the writer himself feels that it is too long, he must do some re-modelling. You cannot break up a long, closely inter-woven sentence into shorter ones simply by planting a full-stop in the middle of it.

No, the stop after 'future' should strictly be a comma, bringing 'methods that would so deeply embitter ...' into its proper relation with 'methods that would only intensify ...'. The only appropriate alternative is a dash, a stop which some pundits refuse to recognize. Personally I regard this as quite a suitable place for it, on the ground that a sentence which might be regarded as complete in itself ('It is not enough ... of the future') is, as it were, picked up and carried on by the repetition of a word ('methods') that has already occurred in it. Moreover, though I have attempted to expose the fallacy of attempting to make punctuation depend sim-ply on the length of a sentence, it must sometimes take account of this, and a dash does seem to relieve the length of a sentence more than a comma does. Try it out and see whether you do not think that a dash here meets the case, for the reasons I have given.

It is not enough to respite the peace of this year by methods that would only intensify the discords and dangers of the future – methods that would so deeply embitter the relations of Britain and Germany as to make their hostility once more incurable . . . etc.

But here am I trespassing on the preserves of the dash out of due order. Returning to the full-stop, I will give one further example of what, with some diffidence this time, I should call its misuse. This one comes from the same highly reputable journal and is provided by a writer for whose style I happen to have a great admiration.

Queues for the unreserved seats stretched a quarter of a mile away to the local greengrocer's. There were little girls in bathing costumes with pails. Homely women with shopping bags. Young misses of sixteen or seventeen, trying to look aloof and sophisticated. Big boys come to see what all the fuss was about. Fathers with families. One child tightly clutching a stuffed model of Dopey. A good-humoured, patient, expectant audience, ready to try today, and to-morrow, and the day after, until at last they could get past the uniformed Cerberus at the door and see for themselves the film they had heard so much about, the film that the management had the 'happy honour to present'.

It may be thought pedantic to raise any objection here, and indeed this is a delightful passage which, even as it stands, cannot very seriously offend anyone's suscepti-bilities. Nobody could want to alter one word of it, but I confess that I do want to alter the punctuation.

It is easy to see what has happened. The writer has deliberately, and quite effectively, dropped for the moment into the 'catalogue' style of writing and has punctuated accordingly. Now, it is one thing to see items set out in catalogue *form*, each on a separate line with a full-stop at the end.

> Latest Spring Models.
> Swim-suits in All Shades.
> Gents' Fancy Vestings.
> Hosiery at Greatly Reduced Prices.

But to introduce a list into what is intended to be read as continuous prose is quite another matter, and I submit that when doing so one should follow the normal rules of punctuation.

In this case the main verb ('There were') on which the whole list depends comes at the very start of it. The writer has put a full-stop after the first item of the list ('little girls . . . with pails'). Then follow five further items, separated by full-stops, not one of which has a finite verb, though in one or two there are participial clauses defining the subject (e.g. 'One child tightly clutching a stuffed model of Dopey'). Last comes, after another full-stop, a passage gathering together all the preceding items into a final summary – 'A good-humoured, patient, expectant audience . . . to present' – which itself has no main verb and cannot stand as an independent sentence.

Actually the whole passage from 'There were . . .' down to '. . . to present' forms a single sentence, however much the writer may attempt to disguise the fact; in construction it is inseparable, for every member of it ultimately depends on the opening 'There were'.

But it is a monster of a sentence, and the writer may well have felt that to put commas in the place of the full-stops would have given it a very cumbersome appearance, liable to put off the reader at a glance. And so it might, though commas here are legitimate and full-stops are not. There is, however, an alternative which would have the effect of lightening this long sentence by breaks rather more substantial than a comma can provide, without breaking it up by full-stops into 'sentences' which are not sentences. When a sentence contains a string of clauses, or of items each composed of several words as opposed to single words, it is perfectly legitimate, and generally most appropriate, to separate these items by semi-colons. Further, in this particular sentence I feel that some different stop at the point where the list ends and the summary begins ('... Dopey. A good-humoured ...') will give the reader a quicker grasp of the construction of the sentence, and thus of its sense. This seems to me, again, just the right place for a dash. Let us, then, have another look at it in its revised form:

Queues for the unreserved seats stretched a quarter of a mile away to the local greengrocer's. There were little girls in bathing costumes with pails; homely women with shopping bags; young misses of sixteen or seventeen, trying to look aloof and sophisticated; big boys come to see what all the fuss was about; fathers with families; one child tightly clutching a stuffed model of Dopey – a good-humoured, patient, expectant audience, ready to try today, and to-morrow, and the day after, until at last they could get past the uniformed Cerberus at the door and see for themselves the film they had heard so much about, the film that the management had the 'happy honour to present'.

By this punctuation we have converted the passage into what it grammatically is, a single sentence. At the same time I maintain that it is not one whit more cumbersome or more difficult for the reader to swallow than in the original. There is no possible room for ambiguity anywhere, and I for one am no longer brought up with an uncomfortable jolt by finding a phrase like 'Fathers with families' posing as an independent sentence, and looking most self-conscious and ungainly in the effort. Nor do I now (as I did at first reading) start the sentence 'A good-humoured . . .' expecting to find a main verb and, finding none, suffer a momentary delay in catching the writer's drift. I submit, in fact, that by sticking to the ordinary rules of punctuation we have helped rather than hindered the reader – and what else is punctuation for?

By way of comparison let me quote here another passage by the same writer, peppered with full-stops just as liberally, but this time quite correctly.

When the talkies came into existence ten years ago there were very few forms of popular entertainment to dispute their authority. They were new. They were exciting. They introduced fresh and stimulating personalities to the public. Things are very different today. There are other entertainments that are newer, and just as exciting. There is dog-racing. There are football pools. There is ice-skating and ice-hockey. There is television and radio.

In this case the punctuation nowhere conflicts with grammatical construction. The words placed between full-stops, even when they number no more than three, form a complete sentence every time. I welcome the opportunity of quoting this extract without any sort of adverse criticism because I realize that some of my remarks, particularly under the heading of The Semi-Colon later on, may give the impression that I have a bee in my bonnet on the subject of jerkiness and disjointedness. This style of writing, if pursued for a page or so on end, would of course become tiresome, but I can appreciate as well as anybody that a series of short, sharp sentences can be very effective in the proper place. When reading this paragraph in its context I did not find it in the least inappropriate or irritating.

To the general rule that whatever intervenes between any two full-stops should be a sentence in the grammatical sense of the word, i.e. should contain at least one main clause having a finite verb, there is one obvious exception. In conversation questions are continually asked or answered by single words, or by three or four words that do not amount to a sentence or even a clause. Naturally in this case the written word corresponds exactly with the spoken word in the abruptness of its stops.

'Now with what part of ourselves do we see visible objects?'

'With the eye-sight.'

'In the same way we hear sounds with the hearing and perceive everything sensible with the other senses, do we not?'

'Certainly.'

'Then have you noticed with what transcendent costliness the architect of the senses has wrought out the faculty of seeing and being seen?'

'Not exactly.'

So in writing that is not actually conversational a

short phrase closely related to the sentence immediately preceding it can similarly stand 'on its own' with a full-stop after it. As often as not, however, instances of this type also will be found in question-and-answer form.

In admitting this much, we do not plead guilty of having been mistaken in our attitude from the start. Far from it.

Are we to assume that these facts justify us in taking a pessimistic view of the situation? Not by any means.

Can the Government be relied upon to act promptly and with decisive effect? Undoubtedly.

The use of the full-stop in abbreviating need not detain us long. It is customary to use a full-stop at the end of an abbreviated word, just as it is used after an initial letter that stands for a whole word, e.g. (there's one – or rather, two) 'inst.', 'Feb.', 'Rev.', 'Maj.-Gen.' etc. (there's another). But there is now a growing tendency to drop the full-stop if the abbreviation consists of simply the first and last letters of the word abbreviated, e.g. 'Mr', 'Dr', and the like. Indeed the author of *Modern English Usage*★ advocates omission of the full-stop whenever the first and last letters of the abbreviation are also the first and last letters of the full word, however many letters the abbreviation may consist of – e.g. Bart, not Bart., for Baronet; Cpl or Corpl for Corporal (but Capt. for Captain). This practice has been adopted by, amongst others, certain of the University Presses, but not by *The Times*, in which even 'Mr.' and 'Dr.' are still so printed. There are some who follow the rule laid down in *Modern English Usage* but

★ *Modern English Usage* by H. W. Fowler (Oxford, Clarendon Press, 1926).

admit one exception, that of inserting a full-stop when the abbreviation is itself a pronounceable word: e.g. 'Cpl' and 'Bt', but 'Bart.' (there is, indeed, something to be said for making a Coy. Commander distinguishable from a Coy Commander).

Another usage connected with the full-stop can also be dealt with very briefly. Three full-stops in combination are used to mark the point where words are omitted in a quotation. Several instances of this may be found within the last few pages, wherever I have thought it necessary to repeat only the beginning and end, or the first few words, of a sentence from a previous quotation. This symbol is also occasionally convenient in ordinary narration when something is left for the reader's imagination to supply. For instance, one could imagine a paragraph descriptive of a meeting of two friends or lovers ending: 'There for the moment let us leave them, talking far into the night ...'. One famous English author made a habit of ending almost every paragraph in this fashion, though the problem of what is to be supplied might often defy even the most lively imagination. Apart from its use in quotations, or to denote stumbling or excited speech ('I never thought ... I can hardly believe ... it is really true that he has come back?'), this symbol is seldom very helpful.

One final point about the full-stop is perhaps the concern rather of the printer than of anybody else. Single words or phrases displayed as headings or at the foot of notices, and so on, used normally to be followed by full-stops.

NOTICE.   MENU.
PROGRAMME OF MUSIC.

BY ORDER OF THE COUNCIL.

CHAPTER FIVE.
THE SNAKE IN THE GRASS.

Modern taste tends to dispense with the full-stop in such cases – rightly, so it seems to me, for when words or phrases are isolated, a stop has no useful purpose to fulfil.

THE COLON. – There are a good many people who seem to regard the colon and the semi-colon as identical stops and who use them both indiscriminately. Others, again, have a strong preference for one and have no use for the other. And indeed, if regard be paid to tradition, it is by no means easy to see exactly how these two stops differ in usage. Take, for instance, this passage from the Old Testament:

And Elisha came again to Gilgal: and there was a dearth in the land; and the sons of the prophets were sitting before him: and he said unto his servant, Set on the great pot, and seethe pottage for the sons of the prophets.

Or, again, compare these two extracts:

The Lord seeth not as man seeth; for man looketh on the outward appearance, but the Lord looketh on the heart.

And the Lord said, Arise, anoint him: for this is he.

I confess that after the most careful observation I still fail to see what principle of differentiation, if any, governs the use of these two stops in the Bible, though one might possibly detect a fraction more 'weight' in the colon than in the semi-colon. The form of the two stops would certainly lead one to suppose that, by origin, the colon approximates more nearly to the full-stop and the semi-colon to the comma. I fancy, however, that one would not be far wrong in saying that for a century or two these stops were used almost indiscriminately.

That two different stops should fulfil precisely the same function is hardly logical, and I have no doubt that they ought to be differentiated and that in the best modern usage they generally are. Nowadays the job of acting as 'half-way house' between the comma and the full-stop has come to devolve more and more on the semi-colon, leaving to the colon only one rather specialized use. This use is much easier to explain by illustration than by definition, though the author of *Modern English Usage* picturesquely defines the function of the colon as 'that of delivering the goods that have been invoiced in the preceding words'. Here, then, are a few illustrations:

The following articles were found in his pockets: a wallet containing three ten-shilling notes, five shillings and four-pence in small change, an empty brandy-flask, a tobacco-pouch, two pipes, and a match-box.

My circumstances were different from what they had been before: I was now a married man with a home of my own, and all the responsibilities that marriage demands.

When the door had been forced open, a scene of indescribable confusion was revealed: drawers rifled, chairs overturned, pictures smashed, and the floor littered with broken glass and crockery.

The chief exports of this flourishing little country are: coal, copper, lead, nitrate, wheat, wool, and timber.

It will be noticed that in the last example the colon

might be dispensed with, for the sentence would run perfectly well: 'The chief exports of this flourishing little country are coal, copper. . .'. But those who prefer to can properly use a colon there, and if the opening clause had ended 'are these', or 'are the following', one could hardly do without it. In fact this use of the colon is inseparably connected with the *idea* of 'namely' or 'as follows', even if those actual words do not occur. In the second and third examples above, for instance, the idea is implicit, even though the writers have not said in so many words (respectively), '*namely that* I was now . . .' and '*the following* scene . . .'.

Thus the colon can be appropriately used to separate a clause that introduces a list, quotation, summary, or corollary from the actual list etc. itself. I would go so far as to say that it is only in this type of context that the colon can be properly used nowadays, though some might quarrel with me for not including its use with contrasted clauses (see p. 38); and that consequently it will be needed rather less often than the semi-colon.*
There is therefore nothing further to be said about it, except to note that the colon and dash are sometimes

---

*I originally wrote this before the appearance of an amusing and persuasive article on 'The Colon' by A.P.H. in *Punch*. Sir Alan is (or was) satisfied that in the Bible the pause made by the colon is more marked than that made by the semi-colon. I can see this distinction better in his supporting quotations than in mine. Still less am I convinced that this subtle difference in 'pause-value' has survived or deserves to do so. The proportion of writers of the present century who so indicate it, and of readers who recognize it, must be very small indeed – and, after all, do we really need two degrees of pause intermediate between the comma and the full-stop?

combined (:—) as a single stop. This usage, however, is declining and is anyhow usually limited to cases where the quotation etc. that follows starts on a fresh line. For instance, in introducing the four examples above I might have written on p. 35

Here, then, are a few illustrations:—

But to have substituted : — for : in any of the examples themselves would have been inappropriate, the colon-and-dash being nowadays generally accounted too formal and fussy for use within a sentence. [See also p. 79.]

THE SEMI-COLON. – There are those who have a prejudice against the semi-colon; personally I find it a very useful stop.

In this opening sentence I have illustrated one of its normal uses. It is heavier than a comma but less heavy than a full-stop, and it comes in handy for separating two sentences which could stand independently with a full-stop between them, but which are somewhat closely connected in sense. In the opening sentence a comma would have been incorrect, because there is no conjunction between the two clauses; if I had joined them by 'but', then I could have punctuated '. . . prejudice against the semi-colon, but personally . . .'. On the other hand a full-stop after 'semi-colon' would have been perfectly legitimate, but it would have produced a rather more jerky effect than I wanted here. Though each half of the statement is actually a sentence complete in itself, I wanted to link them together as closely as possible without the actual use of a conjunction; hence the semi-colon. I need give only one or two more examples to illustrate the use of this stop to separate sentences closely related to each other in sense but not linked by any conjunction.

The candidate could not be said to give a very good impression; he looked as though he needed a good wash.

The German machine-gunners were most difficult to dislodge; they held out to the end with complete devotion.

In both these instances the semi-colon could quite properly have been replaced by a full-stop, but the effect might have been a little too jerky and disjointed, especially if the context provided other short sentences immediately before or after. On the other hand the semi-colons could *not* have been replaced by commas unless conjunctions were inserted – in the first example '... good impression, *since* he looked ...'; in the second '... difficult to dislodge, *and* they held out ...'. (Note that in this latter case a comma between two simple clauses joined by 'and' is unnecessary and is better omitted altogether.) The authors, however, may have felt that with conjunctions the sentences would lose too much of their crispness, and the semi-colon thus provides just the right compromise. It is also frequently used between two evenly balanced sentences that strike a contrast, where a conjunction would make the contrast less pointed. e.g.

All the virtue and all the praise go to Socialism; all that is unvirtuous and damnable is non-Socialist.

(This is a type of context in which some would even today use the colon. Admittedly it was used in this way by the writers of the Authorized Version, and it is invariably used in Latin to mark a contrast, so that the Latin colon often *means* 'but'. Still, this task is allotted more often to the semi-colon in modern English.)

A semi-colon can also be combined with a conjunction, but this use needs rather careful discrimination. Let us take some concrete examples to see how it works out.

(i) He could not get up, so he rolled to the trench and fell in; but before he would be carried off to have his painful injuries cared for, he gave directions for the prosecution of the counter-attack.

(ii) He collected a miscellaneous force consisting largely of cooks, batmen, lorry-drivers, men returning from leave, and other details; and these troops managed to hold back the enemy till nightfall.

(iii) When they reached the frontier, they were deprived of their tickets, their passports, and their heavy luggage; so there they had to stay.

(iv) Dropping his bundle without a moment's hesitation, he turned and ran; because he knew it would be fatal to do otherwise.

(v) Few would agree that this is the best policy; since it would inevitably lead to war.

In all these instances a semi-colon is interposed between sentences or clauses that are joined by conjunctions. In none of them, consequently, would a full-stop be an appropriate substitute (so long, of course, as the conjunction is retained). In the first three examples it would be legitimate, but would produce a disjointed effect, especially unpleasant in (ii). In (iv) and

(v) it would be definitely wrong, because in each case the stop is followed by a subordinate clause and not by a sentence which could at a pinch stand independently. On the other hand a comma would be a legitimate substitute in every case. There are, however, perfectly sound reasons for preferring semi-colons in the first three examples. In all three there are commas at various other points in the sentences, and at the particular point at which the semi-colon is used the sense calls for a slightly more pronounced pause than at the comma-points. This is particularly noticeable in (ii), where a semi-colon even precedes an 'and'.

In the last two examples the semi-colons are incorrect, or (if that sounds too dogmatic) at the very least quite inappropriate. In each instance the clause following the semi-colon depends very closely on the clause preceding it, so that the semi-colon makes the break between them too marked. Commas at 'ran' in (iv) and 'policy' in (v) would give all the break that is needed.

Thus in using semi-colons to mark off clauses introduced by conjunctions, it is necessary to distinguish between conjunctions that *co-ordinate* ('and', 'or', 'but', 'yet' etc.) and those that *subordinate* ('as', 'since', 'because', 'when', 'if', 'though' etc.). Whereas there will be plenty of instances in which a semi-colon can appropriately be used immediately before a co-ordinate clause, because an extra pause is needed, there will be precious few, if any, in which it will suit a subordinate clause, since the latter, being closely *dependent* on the main clause, generally needs to be closely linked with it. Can you imagine any 'when' or 'if' clause, for instance, with which a semi-colon would be tolerable?

I should like to have a look at that book; when you have quite done with it.

The game would inevitably have ended in a draw and a re-play would have been necessary; if one of the full-backs had not lost his head just before the end and handled the ball.

Scarcely ever will it work with any subordinate conjunction, though certain writers make a habit of using it in this perverse way. Therefore it is a sound rule to eschew semi-colons before subordinate clauses, but to use them with co-ordinate clauses wherever they really aid the sense.

Semi-colons may also be used to separate phrases, as opposed to sentences or clauses, if these phrases are somewhat lengthy, and especially if there are already commas to mark slighter pauses within the phrases themselves. Actually I have already shown this on pp. 29–30 *à propos* of the full-stop, but two more examples may not be out of place here.

(i) Slipping and floundering for hours at a snail's pace through mud and slime, long files of men went to and fro – carrying-parties with food, water, ammunition of all kinds, engineer and ordnance stores; forward observation parties with their wire and telephone equipment; stretcher-parties piteously burdened; reliefs bulky with arms and full pack and perhaps a parcel from home, struggling after the lightly loaded guide.

(Incidentally notice the use of the dash in this extract. It corresponds almost exactly with its suggested use on p. 29, but here the 'summary' comes first and the separate 'items' follow it; in the other passage the order was reversed. Here a colon might have been used instead, but I can see no other possible alternative.)

(ii) The strikers agreed to resume work immediately if a tribunal were formed to investigate their grievances; if on such tribunal the workers were adequately represented; if an undertaking were given that there would not, either now or at any future time, be any victimization; and finally if it were guaranteed that, when the recommendations of the tribunal were announced, they would be put into force without delay.

The appropriateness and convenience of the semi-colons in both these passages will surely be obvious. They cannot be replaced by full-stops, because in (i) they separate a series of phrases, none of which contains a finite verb, and in (ii) they separate a series of subordinate clauses. They could be replaced by commas, but the result would be confusing. In (i) we have a list of items of which the 'long files of men' consist. Each of these items is of some length, amounting sometimes to more than a dozen words and already containing commas. The first item includes a second list of its own – 'food, water . . .' etc. – separated by commas. Another comma after 'stores' would get the 'forward observation parties' inextricably mixed up with the various burdens of the 'carrying-parties', and if a semi-colon is consequently needed at the end of the first item, then for the sake of clearness the same stop should come at the end of each of the other component parts of the 'long files'. The sentence in fact simply asks for semi-colons if the reader is to grasp its meaning instantly. Punctuated in any other way it might be thoroughly confusing, but as it stands it cannot present the slightest difficulty to anyone.

The use of commas for semi-colons in (ii) would have no such unfortunate result, but semi-colons are to be preferred simply because the clauses they separate are rather lengthy and some of them contain commas of their own. Thus the semi-colons serve to pick out a little more clearly the conditions on which 'the strikers agreed to resume work immediately'; and this in fact should always be the governing factor in choosing between commas and semi-colons to separate strings of parallel clauses or phrases. The semi-colon is preferable if it is going to help the reader's eye, and the circumstances in which it is likely to do so are when the clauses or phrases are themselves rather long, or when they already contain commas.

Lest an undiscriminating reader should jump to the conclusion that in this second example, by leaving one or two 'if' clauses marooned between semi-colons, I have contradicted a statement I made on p. 41, perhaps I had better point out that we are now dealing with something quite different. This is a question of separating a string of 'if' clauses from each other. Each of them depends on the main verb 'agreed (to resume work)', and it may be noticed that the 'if' clause nearest to it is not separated from it even by a comma.

We have now, I hope, had enough of the semi-colon. I have shown that, being less than a full-stop and more than a comma, it can be used in place sometimes of the one and sometimes of the other. I have tried to explain the conditions appropriate to its use, and I hope that I have succeeded in establishing its respectability. While it is possible to get on without it, there are times and places in which it comes in very handy.

3

THE LIGHTER STOPS

Comma – Brackets – Dash

'TAKE care of the pence and the pounds will take care of themselves' is a common proverb. It would be almost equally true to say 'Take care of the commas and the other stops will take care of themselves', for the writer who handles this puny little stop correctly and sensibly can probably punctuate as well as need be.

The first and most obvious point to emphasize about the comma is that it should not be so inserted as to cause an unnecessary break in the construction of the sentence. I have illustrated this point very briefly in my introductory chapter (p. 16) by mispunctuating a sentence that appeared correctly in *The Times*. Here are some further instances in which the mispunctuation belongs not to me but to the original book or periodical.

(i) Strangest of all the new sensations, was this uprising of physical virility.

(ii) It seems simpler to take one's passport, or, to acquire one.

(iii) Martin, never by the flicker of an eyelid, gave an emotion away.

(iv) The proposals which, it is believed, Mr Chamberlain is taking with him, are set out in an adjoining column.

(v) No praise could be too high for the manner in which W. J. O'Reilly, who confirmed his claim to be regarded as the best bowler in the world, and L. O'B. Fleetwood-Smith, had toiled away while England's score grew and grew.

(vi) The exact words used by Lord Beaconsfield as I remember clearly were:—'Lord Salisbury and I have brought you back peace, and, a peace, I hope not without honour.'

In (i) and (iii) the commas interrupt the run of straightforward sentences, and that's that. In (ii) the comma before 'or' can be justified (as marking a kind of afterthought); the one after it cannot. In (iv) and (v) it is possible that relative clauses (as often happens) have had some hand in confusing the issue. In (iv) the comma after 'him' would be legitimate, and in fact necessary, if there had been a comma also after 'proposals' bracketing off, as it were, the whole relative clause 'which [it is believed] Mr Chamberlain is taking with him'. But the writer, by omitting a comma after 'proposals', has made this a *defining* relative clause, requiring no comma at either end (explained fully on pp. 55–7). Therefore the comma after 'him' becomes an interruption. In (v) there is a relative clause after 'O'Reilly' which is quite properly marked off by commas at beginning and end, and treating it as comfortably tucked away as though in brackets we are left with the main clause:

. . . the manner in which W. J. O'Reilly and L. O'B. Fleetwood-Smith, had toiled away. . . .

The comma after 'Fleetwood-Smith' is thus exposed as an obvious intruder.

The sixth extract demands a short paragraph to itself, for it strikes me as a prize instance of comma-spraying indulged in without rhyme or reason. Assuming that no two of the commas are to be paired, you get an effect of breaks that do not correspond with the sense, thus (I use lines for commas simply to make the point a little more obvious):

Lord S. and I have brought you back peace | and | a peace | I hope not without honour.

If you try pairing any of the commas bracket-wise, the result is nonsensical:

. . . have brought you back peace (and) a peace, I hope not without honour.

. . . have brought you back peace, and (a peace) I hope not without honour.

On the other hand there *are* words ('I hope') that need to be bracketed off by commas; and while we are at it we may as well note that in the first clause the word 'clearly' might, as things stand, be taken with either 'remember' or 'were'. The extract is from a letter contributed to *The Times*, so perhaps the correspondent, and not the editor, should be held responsible for not punctuating as follows:

The exact words used by Lord Beaconsfield, as I remember clearly, were: 'Lord Salisbury and I have brought you back peace, and a peace, I hope, not without honour.'

While misuse of the comma comes mostly from putting it in where no stop is needed, one very common fault is of the opposite kind, namely the use of a comma where a *heavier* stop is needed, and I intend to dispose of that next.

(i) The dog is a very faithful animal, it will usually do anything for its master.

(ii) The rain began to come down heavily, I was soon wet through.

(iii) To proceed was impossible, the road was blocked by an overturned lorry.

Here we are dealing – from the other side of the fence, so to speak – with exactly the same point as was discussed on pp. 37–8. I come back to it from this end because the commonest form of 'schoolboy' mistake is to separate by a comma two clauses that are not linked by a conjunction. Schoolboys, however, are not the only sinners in this respect; plenty of others do it habitually, and some of them no doubt would be prepared to defend this practice. I obstinately hold to the view that it is slovenly and will not do. The same treatment applies to the three sentences given above as to the examples quoted on p. 38. If (assuming you are the writer) you prefer not to join by conjunctions the two clauses of which each of the sentences is composed, you must separate them either by a full-stop or a semi-colon; a comma is not a heavy enough stop to 'carry' the break which you have chosen to make by the mere form of your sentence. Which of the two former stops you use should depend on how closely the two clauses are related in sense and on the particular effect you wish to produce. Personally I should vote for a semi-colon in (i) because of the close connection. A full-stop would do perfectly well in (ii) and (iii) if a certain abruptness suited the context; if it did not, I should probably go the whole hog, especially in (ii), and join up the two halves by a conjunction.

I am going to repeat those sentences so joined, because that will introduce my next point – the insertion or omission of commas with conjunctions.

The rain began to come down heavily and I was soon wet through.

To proceed was impossible, for [as, since, because] the road was blocked by an overturned lorry.

In the former sentence, in which two short and closely related clauses are joined by 'and', a comma after 'heavily' is clearly unnecessary. In the latter, in which the second clause is subordinate to the first, a comma after 'impossible' is normal, though not essential. We are getting into the realm where rules begin to give way to personal taste, but in general it may be said that a comma is out of place before 'and' and 'or' when they join two (and not more than two) words, phrases, or short clauses; before any other conjunction joining two clauses it is quite legitimate and often helpful. We cannot make quite the same clean-cut distinction between co-ordinate and subordinate conjunctions here as was applied on p. 40; for whereas 'and' and 'but' are both co-ordinate conjunctions, the former simply links, while the latter contrasts. Hence a comma (or even a semi-colon) is usually appropriate before 'but', seldom before 'and'.

I have read that book and I like it very much.

I have read that book, but I do not like it very much.

It is in fact neither possible nor desirable to lay down any hard-and-fast rule about this sort of thing. Modern economy in punctuation is tending towards the omission of commas even with subordinate clauses where no ambiguity can result (and occasionally where it can, as shown on pp. 68 and 123); whilst on the other hand prevention of ambiguity, and sometimes the mere length of a sentence (see p. 17), may demand the insertion of a comma before 'and'. The exact degree of pause required by the particular context is also a factor to be reckoned with. An assortment of examples, with some comments to follow, will probably be more useful than any attempt to dogmatize.

(i) It is impossible, and indeed undesirable, to lay down hard-and-fast rules on this subject.

(ii) I stayed with him most of the afternoon and next day, on going to see him again, found him a little better.

(iii) In this game it is best to cut down your contacts and work, as far as possible, alone.

(iv) The true background behind him this morning is that the negotiations in Prague have not as yet been broken off, and that no reasonable solution which he might be thought to support need be ruled out of the discussion.

(v) Her style of dress was smart but not gaudy.

(vi) The favourite at that point was in the third place but was still full of running.

(vii) Recoiling to the Wytschaete crest, the defence firmly held on, and no impression was made on the British line at Hollebeke; but Messines was lost in the night after a day of stern struggle.

(viii) If therefore the Prime Minister refuses Mr Attlee's request, it will certainly not be because the Government do not wish to face the House of Commons.

(ix) In any case no settlement is worth having if it is calculated to last for no more than a matter of months.

(x) This news, if it can be relied upon, is highly significant.

(xi) When bread and other provisions ran short, they ate dwarf cactus, guanacos and birds, and all the while they lived in dread of the Indians, the gigantic Patagonians they had heard about. When the Indians finally appeared the meeting was a friendly one, marred but once by tragedy when three settlers were killed by the natives.

(xii) I am doing this because I must.

(xiii) Don't go on telling me that, because I have heard it often enough already.

(xiv) Life today is not so much a checker-board of blacks and whites, as a kind of universal grey in which men are groping blindly and half-heartedly for some guiding thread of light.

(xv) I believe that the trouble today is that life is so complex and the issues so involved and obscure, that men find it hard to see which way their duty lies.

In (i) the comma before 'and' reinforces 'indeed' in adding a stress to the second epithet ('undesirable') that it would not have had in the simple form 'It is impossible and undesirable to lay down . . .'. Note that the insertion of this comma makes a second one after 'undesirable' necessary.

Both (ii) and (iii) are ambiguous as they stand because the reader might momentarily couple in (ii) 'the afternoon and next day', and in (iii) 'contacts and work', partly because of the commas required after 'day' and 'work'. The principle that the reader must never, even for a moment, be led astray demands a comma before each 'and'.

(iv) provides an instance of a comma being used before 'and' presumably because of the length of the two clauses which the 'and' joins. It is purely optional here, though perhaps desirable as a breath-pause.

(v) and (vi) are instances of 'but' without so much as a comma before it. In (v) the 'but' merely joins a couple of epithets in contrast. In (vi) there would be no objection to a comma after 'place', but the two clauses, sharing the same subject, are so closely related in sense that it can quite well be spared. In (vii), on the other hand, the writer felt the need of a stop even heavier than a comma before 'but', no doubt because of the length of the previous clause, which moreover has commas of its own (though the one after 'on' is not absolutely necessary), and because a little extra break before the last clause is consistent with the sense and helps to mark a contrast.

The next half-dozen instances are intended to illustrate how much the insertion or omission of commas to mark off subordinate clauses seems to have become a matter of personal taste. (viii) and (ix) are taken from consecutive leading articles in *The Times*; the former has a comma between the 'if' clause and the main clause, but the latter has none. Perhaps a comma can be dispensed with more readily when the 'if' clause follows the main clause than when it precedes it, but I should hesitate to stake too much on that distinction. When, however, the 'if' clause (or any other kind of subordinate clause) is sandwiched into the main clause, as in (x), a pair of commas used bracket-wise at the beginning and end of the subordinate clause becomes almost essential.

In (xi) a comma is inserted at the end of a 'when' clause that starts the first sentence but not at the end of another one starting the very next sentence, though both are in exactly the same kind of context. 'You pays your money and you takes your choice' – but it is as well to be at any rate consistent. Note too that the distinction tentatively suggested concerning 'if' clauses really does apply to 'when' clauses, as instanced by the third 'when' clause in this passage: i.e. where the 'when' clause follows the main clause the comma can more easily be dispensed with than where the order is the reverse. To give a very simple instance, in 'When I heard the news, I was greatly distressed' the comma does not intrude, but in 'I was greatly distressed, when I heard the news' it does.

In (xii) and (xiii) there is a slight distinction in sense to warrant the omission of the comma in the one case and its insertion in the other. In the former sentence the 'because' clause is much more closely bound up with the sense of the main clause than in the latter.

The commas in (xiv) and (xv) are superfluous according to modern usage, though the extracts are from a contemporary writer. In an earlier age it was normal to punctuate 'It is not so much a crime, as a foolish blunder'; 'He was so tall, that he could easily see over the heads of the crowd'; and so on. It is probably true to say that immediately before the conjunction 'that' a comma will be admissible more rarely than before any other conjunction – you have only to look at the first seven words of this sentence in order to find one of the commonest uses of 'that' and to realize how unnecessary is a comma in such contexts. (It should perhaps be added that in (xv) a comma after 'complex' would justify the one after 'obscure' and would accord with modern usage.)

So much for the combination of comma and conjunction. I have shown, I hope, that the insertion or omission of the comma must depend in the main on whether the sense does or does not require a slight break and on the need to avoid ambiguity. Now for what seem to me the most important of the many other uses and abuses of the comma.

Participial Clauses, whether occurring at the beginning or end of a sentence, or within it, are usually closed or prefaced by, or enclosed between, commas. e.g.

Sitting down, he opened his newspaper.

He put down his paper and, turning to me, inquired what I thought of the situation.

He buried himself once more in his newspaper, having tired of the conversation.

Notice a slight but common error in this connection:

He found a match, and bending over, struck it on the floor.

She dismounted, and leaving her bicycle on the turf, began to walk up an ascending track.

In order to mark the start of the participial clauses, the commas should follow instead of preceding the 'ands' – here merely a matter of transposing. If there must anyhow be a break between the two main verbs, then an extra comma will be needed:

I tried hard to concentrate, but, being utterly exhausted, fell asleep.

There is another connection in which the position of the comma in participial clauses needs special care.

Yorkshire, having already won the Championship, their match against Sussex yesterday at Hove lost something of its importance.

This punctuation (from a leading daily paper) offends against syntax. Here 'Yorkshire' is actually an inseparable part of the participial clause, from which the comma has automatically excluded it. The point may seem a trivial one, but to a reader with any feeling for grammar this abuse of the comma is definitely misleading. The comma after 'Yorkshire' makes him expect to find that word acting as subject to the main clause, in some such way as this:

Yorkshire, having already won the Championship, could afford to take their match with Sussex less seriously than they would otherwise have done.

When instead he is suddenly brought up against a new subject ('their match') to the main clause, he has a moment's doubt whether he has read the sentence aright and starts it again. If the sentence had been punctuated

Yorkshire having already won the Championship, their match against Sussex . . .

he would have seen at a glance that 'Yorkshire' was safely tucked away in the participial clause and would have been ready for any fresh subject that the writer chose to introduce. We are dealing with the equivalent in English of our old friend the Ablative Absolute in Latin.

The enemy having been defeated [*Abl. Abs.*], our men captured the city.

The enemy [*Nominative Subject*], having been defeated [*Nom. in agreement with Subj.*], retired beyond the river.

But whereas Latin marks the difference in construction by an altered case-ending, English has to do so with nothing but a comma, which thus has a big responsibility in sentences of this type.

In *Relative Clauses* also a clear distinction in sense is marked by the insertion or omission of a comma before the relative pronoun.

(i) The facts which he stated were quite conclusive.

(ii) He acquainted me with the facts, which he stated with scrupulous fairness.

(iii) I became aware that my pursuer, who by now was only a few yards off, was the man whom I had seen that morning at the inn.

In (i) the relative clause defines the particular facts that were quite conclusive, namely the ones 'which he stated', and thus it is really an essential part of the sentence. In (ii) the relative clause adds to the main clause a fresh point about the 'facts' that is not essential to the sense; it does not define the facts themselves but describes something about the statement of them. Similarly in (iii) the first relative clause describes something about the 'pursuer', whilst the second one defines, or identifies, the man. This distinction in sense between two types of relative clause, which Fowler★ labels *defining* and *non-defining* (sometimes termed *descriptive*), needs to be marked by a distinction in punctuation: no comma with *defining*, comma before (and after if necessary, as (iii) above) *non-defining*.

Some authorities insist that the substitution of 'that' for 'who', 'whom', 'which' (e.g. in (i) and (iii) on p. 55 'The facts that...' and 'the man that...') should mark the distinction. And indeed it should; but this practice will not cover 'whose' 'by which', etc., not to mention 'where' and 'when', whereas punctuation can do it invariably. Yet it is remarkable how little trouble is taken, even by good writers, over this comma-distinction. There is room here for only very few examples:

(i) There is a very small staff which is never idle.

(ii) *Eminent Victorians*, the first of his books, in which he set a precedent for ironic and detached biography ...

(iii) When he spoke he did so through his teeth which gave his words a flavour of precision.

In all these the true meaning is distorted: in (i) by omission of comma ('... small staff, which [= and it] is never idle' – otherwise the implication is that the majority of the staff *is* idle); in (ii) by insertion of comma before 'in which' (this was not the first of Strachey's books, but the first to comprise 'ironic...biography'); in (iii) by omission of comma (it was not his teeth, but the fact that he spoke through them, that gave the 'flavour of precision' – 'which' = 'a thing [fact] which' can indeed never be *defining* and must always have a

★ *Modern English Usage* (1926), p. 635.

preceding comma). In short, the relative clause of (ii) defines; the other two do not – they describe.

The use of the comma with certain *Single Words or Short Phrases*, such as 'however', 'meanwhile', 'nevertheless', etc., calls for some comment. Once again it will probably be best to illustrate first and discuss afterwards.

(i) However the incident may be explained, the impression it has left is unfortunate.

(ii) However, the incident may be explained in such a way as to satisfy public opinion.

(iii) These incidents, however, trivial in themselves, are liable to lead to more serious demonstrations.

(iv) Meanwhile the situation is steadily deteriorating.

(v) Meanwhile, unless the Government takes firm action, the situation will steadily deteriorate.

(vi) Nevertheless reinforcements and supplies were brought up to the front line during the height of the bombardment.

(vii) None the less, reinforcements and supplies were brought up . . . etc.

(viii) No doubt the state of the wicket had something to do with the smallness of the score.

(ix) He had, no doubt, a speech carefully prepared for the occasion.

(x) If the success was due chiefly to the backs, the forwards too played their part very creditably.

(xi) Full account must be taken, too, of the strength of the opposition which they had to encounter.

There is a not uncommon tendency to 'comma off' all such words and phrases. I can see no necessity for doing so with words that can only be used 'absolutely', or, shall we say, that cannot take on a slightly different meaning if closely combined with some other word or words. 'Meanwhile' is such a one, in contrast with 'however', which, as the first example shows, has more than a mere 'absolute' use; note, too, the alteration of sense that would result in (iii) from the omission of the comma after 'however'. To save possible confusion it is a sound practice to put a comma after 'however' (and before as well, if it is not the first word of its clause) whenever it is used absolutely; but no such consideration applies to 'meanwhile'. It is quite unnecessary to put a comma after it, as is often done, in such sentences as (iv), or indeed in any other. The comma that follows it in (v) does not, so to speak, belong to the 'meanwhile' at all; it belongs to the subordinate clause ('unless . . . action'), which, sandwiched into the main clause, needs to be marked off by a comma at the beginning and end – our old friends the 'bracket-commas' again.

I see no need for comma after 'nevertheless', but if 'none the less' is used instead of it there may be a slight risk of ambiguity; hence the comma in (vii). (viii) and (ix) illustrate a similar point with 'no doubt'. The general principle I would recommend is to 'comma off' all words and phrases when the omission of commas might momentarily mislead, as in (ii), (iii), (vii), and (ix) above, but not otherwise.

Again, there is no need for 'too' to be enclosed within commas (as it commonly is) unless, as in (xi), it qualifies a statement as a whole. When it belongs to a single word (the 'forwards', in (x), in contrast to the 'backs'), the commas 'too' is apt to attract merely get in the way. Exactly the same applies to 'also'.

In fact if there is one respect in which modern usage tends to be profuse with unnecessary commas, it is with adverbs and adverbial phrases. Let it be granted that a writer may need the comma in order to convey a precise shade of meaning (e.g. reservation, emphasis, afterthought), as in:

I regard them, normally, as superfluous.

He denied it, categorically and indignantly.

I am prepared to put up with the inconvenience, for the time being.

Or again, it may help to steer the reader clear of being momentarily misled through its absence:

Outside, the house looked bleak and sinister.

In the evening, paper lanterns were floated down the seven rivers of Hiroshima.

But consider the following, which for sheer futility can be matched a hundredfold every day of the week:

(i) There were people in the streets, already.

(ii) The match was for some time level but, eventually, the visitors weakened.

(iii) Devoutly, she hoped he would go away.

(iv) In December, she would be sixteen.

(v) From Moukden, I returned to Peking.

(vi) The world today has no more room for him and, in a few years, his type will be extinct.

(vii) The door was open and, by the light from inside, he could see the figure of the intruder.

(viii) What Chesterton, in *The Secret People*, made the English say, can, today, with far greater dramatic significance, be put into the mouths of the Africans.

Half of these call for no comment; (ii), (vi), and (vii), however, show how this adverbial magnet is apt to draw commas away from positions where they may be more needed. Thus:

(ii) The match was for some time level, but eventually the visitors weakened.

(vi) . . . has no more room for him, and in a few years his type . . .

(vii) The door was open, and by the light from inside he could see . . .

Admittedly (vi) and (vii) could do without any commas, but the revised versions give the only sensible places for them. In (viii) – from *The Times*, alas – is a whole crop of superfluous commas. The sentence could do without any at all, but perhaps would read best as:

What Chesterton in *The Secret People* made the English say can today, with far greater dramatic singificance, be put into the mouths of the Africans.

Finally, from the discreet columns of an *Observer* 'Profile', an instance of this fetish inviting actual misapprehension:

. . . one of those . . . who never lost an opportunity, never frittered their time away, but always knew exactly what they wanted and planned, determinedly, to get it.

At first reading one can hardly avoid coupling 'what they wanted and planned'; the real meaning, however, is:

> . . . always knew exactly what they wanted, and planned determinedly to get it.

Numerals also appear to have an attraction for the unnecessary comma. I do not mean the commas used in order to facilitate reckoning – 3,500,000 and so on. But with dates and addresses, for instance, commas crop up freely, and often, as I think, superfluously:

> On November 11, an armistice was signed.

> During 1956, the wages index rose by 9 or 10 points.

If the numeral is followed by a word that could readily, and wrongly, be attached to it, or by another group of numerals, naturally commas become necessary:

> On November 11, men could begin to breathe more freely again.

> Between 1721 and 1737, 985 new houses were built in Berlin.

Similarly in giving dates in full, commas may be necessary, as:

> On November 11, 1918, an armistice was signed

and even perhaps:

> On November 11th, 1918, . . .

but not in the form:

> On 11 November 1918 an armistice . . .

My chief concern, however, is to unseat the comma

in the type of sentence quoted first in this connection. Equally useless is the comma that continually intrudes in addresses, and my treatment of it would be equally ruthless. What is wrong with '7 Lancaster Gate' and what conceivable object is there in writing '7, Lancaster Gate'? Let us deal with that comma as we would deal with any other gate-crasher.

While I am on the subject of addresses I cannot resist having a tilt at another matter connected with them, though unconnected with commas. There is (or was until lately) a convention in certain quarters of printing the names of streets etc. as 'Regent-street',' Portland-place', 'Shaftesbury-avenue', 'Berkeley-square', and so on. Why 'street', 'road' etc. should in this one connection fail to conform with the normal rule for the use of capitals (see p. 85) has always been a mystery to me; and the insertion of the hyphen seems peculiarly gratuitous. The streets themselves are not labelled in this way, nor do their names generally so appear on advertisements, buses, Underground stations, notepaper-headings, visiting cards, and the like. The thing seems quite pointless; and when we get, for instance, 'Charing Cross-road' –I have seen it printed even 'Charing cross-road' – the result is a silly ambiguity. There are signs that this irritating practice is beginning to decline, so let us hope that 'Regent Street' and 'Shaftesbury Avenue' will soon be the invariable form and that we may say farewell to 'Leicester-square'.

Three simple uses of the comma, involving scarcely any qualification, can be stated very briefly. Words or phrases *In Apposition* to a preceding word or phrase are customarily placed between commas.

Mr Sandys, the Minister of Defence, left for Washington yesterday.

The capture of the eastern edge of the wood, a difficult and costly operation, was completed before nightfall.

In *Addressing* persons, commas are used to mark off the names or titles of the persons addressed.

You will agree with me, gentlemen, that the Company has had a most successful year.

'Is it your wish, sir, to wear the old school tie today?' 'Yes, James, I will.'

When *Two or More Epithets* qualify the same noun, it is usual to separate the epithets by commas if they are, so to speak, cumulative; not otherwise. e.g.

A dazzling, luxurious limousine drew up.

He was a sallow, weedy, insignificant-looking individual.

But

A large grey sports car drew up.

Some ugly new seaside bungalows.

One 'comma problem', on which opinion is divided, must be dealt with fully because, trivial though it may be in itself, it is continually cropping up. When there is a series of items separated by commas, with an 'and' or 'or' linking up the final item, should there or should there not be a comma before the final 'and' (or 'or')? This is the kind of thing I mean:

At what time ye hear the sound of the cornet, flute, harp, sackbut, psaltery, dulcimer, and all kinds of musick.

Those who hold that the final comma is unnecessary because the 'and' is to be regarded as a substitute for the comma may have logic on their side. Yet in this case I for one am not content to be strictly logical, simply because just occasionally an ambiguity, which would never arise if the insertion of that particular comma were habitual, may arise from the practice of omitting it. Take this sentence for example:

The firms involved were Harrods, Barkers, Lyons, Marks and Spencers, and Woolworths.

Punctuated thus, the list of separate firms is perfectly distinct; but adopting the other rule you get:

The firms involved were Harrods, Barkers, Lyons, Marks and Spencers and Woolworths.

How is anyone to know that two of the last three names are combined as one firm, and which two are so combined? It is no good telling me that everybody has heard of Marks and Spencers. Even if familiarity would prevent most of us from going wrong here, this is merely a handy illustration of the *kind* of ambiguity that will occur now and again under the 'no comma' principle but need never occur if you adopt the other principle.

Here is another, authentic, instance:

Five London boroughs ... Barnes, Hammersmith, Brentford and Chiswick, Fulham, and Wandsworth.

Had this been printed with no comma before the final 'and' Fulham and Wandsworth might just as easily be a single borough as Brentford and Chiswick – which would leave you with only four boroughs instead of five, and what was meant to be informative becomes a puzzle.

All this applies equally, of course, when the list or series consists not of single words but of clauses:

His experience of office, his knowledge of affairs, his authority as a world figure, and his wide-ranging genius are unrivalled.

When all is said, this remains a matter for individual choice. But it is also a mattter of general principle; you can belong to the 'final comma school' or the 'no final comma school', but, having made your choice, you should aim at consistency. Because the 'no final comma' principle breaks down now and again through ambiguity, whilst the 'final comma' principle can be followed consistently with less risk of it, I personally vote for the latter. And I have a further reason. When I see a series of words, phrases, or clauses mostly separated by commas, any two of them that happen to be joined together by 'and' without a comma seem, to my eye at any rate, to be thereby brought into closer mutual relationship than the others; and even when the two thus joined happen to be the last two I still have the same instinctive feeling. Nine times out of ten this specially close connection of the two last items is not borne out by the sense, and consequently the effect produced on my mind, through my eye, is wrong. On the other hand if any two items in a list should really be in a specially close relationship, the 'final comma' man, in order to indicate this, has merely to couple them with an 'and' and drop the comma.

He had a large assortment of potted foods – chicken and

tongue, bloater, anchovy, lobster, salmon and shrimp. The 'no comma' man, on the other hand, is properly cornered, having no comma to drop – presumably he must resort to hyphens for his salmon-and-shrimp.

There is, however, an opposite and not very uncommon error to be avoided, that of inserting an *extra* comma between the final item introduced by 'and' and the verb. e.g.

Their peaceful habits, the routine of their uneventful existence, and their quiet gossip, excited her compassion.

The comma after 'gossip' is unwanted. Yet observe that it would be justifiable if the final 'and' were not there; for then the items would stand, as it were, in apposition (see p. 62). Two or three more instances should make this point clearer:

Egypt, Indonesia, India, are least willing to join the Western alliance.

The finer points of style, the music, the subtlety, the aptness, the rhythm, can hardly fail to escape him.

You can't do anything, get anywhere, in this country unless you belong to a trade union.

Here the omission of 'and' or 'or' alters the 'feel' of the sentences, so that now a comma *after* the final item is needed to prevent the unwarranted closer association of that item with the verb that I have tried to describe on p. 65. In the last example the insertion of 'or' would eliminate two commas:

You can't do anything or get anywhere in this country unless . . .

One more point, connected solely with 'or'. When

used, as it most often is, to separate two alternatives, no comma should intervene; but when, as sometimes, it is equivalent to 'in other words', a preceding comma is needed to mark this meaning.

It was thought that he had been killed or injured, but it transpired that he was suffering from amnesia, or loss of memory.

In parting with the comma, on which even more could be said if there were space, I would emphasize again that punctuation, like language, is subject to evolution and that we are more economical in the use of stops than our forefathers were. If anyone sat down today to repunctuate the Bible, he would find himself deleting thousands of superfluous commas and changing hundreds of heavier stops into commas.

If I whet my glittering sword, and mine hand take hold on judgement; I will render vengeance to mine enemies, and will reward them that hate me.

would become

If I whet my glittering sword and mine hand take hold on judgement, I will render vengeance to mine enemies and will reward them that hate me.

The modern tendency towards economy in punctuation (except as exemplified on pp. 57–62 above) does sometimes, however, over-reach itself and lead to ambiguity. Instances such as the following, all from reputable sources, are far from rare:

(i) So far as I knew that poem had never been published.

(ii) As it turned out the Soviet delegation were not prepared to discuss the West's proposals.

(iii) If necessary steps could have been taken to reassure them.

(iv) From the first two principles, I think, have been in conflict in the British mind.

(v) Everyone felt like the Prime Minister himself that in one sense the thing was done.

Each one of these contains something that, at the first glance, is liable to lead the reader astray. A comma after 'knew' in (i), after 'out' in (ii), after 'necessary' in (iii), after 'first' in (iv), and after both 'felt' and 'himself' in (v) would save him from the momentary, and very natural, impulse to link together 'knew that poem', 'turned out the Soviet delegation', 'necessary steps', 'the first two principles', 'felt like the Prime Minister'.*

At its best, however, modern punctuation uses no more stops than are needed to give immediate clarity and force to the sense; and beyond that point it can hardly go. If my treatment of the comma has failed to establish this as my guiding principle, I can do no more now than recommend my readers to make it theirs.

BRACKETS need not detain us long; their use is almost self-evident and should need but little illustration. They introduce into a context something that has a bearing upon it in a purely subordinate way, and their effect is to keep the words that they enclose 'out of the light', as it were, so that the words that precede and follow them may run on with the least possible interruption. Their bearing on the main theme is generally in the nature of an afterthought or a 'by the way' remark, a sudden interjection, a brief explanation, or a reference.

*See also pp. 123–4.

(i) I completed my preliminary survey of Constantinople (as a tripper should) by visiting museums.

(ii) The men are dingy and apathetic, and are probably thinking (if they are thinking at all) about something else.

(iii) The reliefs were to proceed to Hell Fire Corner (name of ill omen!), where further orders would be issued to them.

(iv) The 'pueblos' (towns or villages) are still as they were years ago.

(v) I shall have more to say on this subject later on (see p. 277).

The only common error connected with the use of brackets arises out of the association of other stops with them; for instance, it would not be unexampled to find (ii) punctuated '... are probably thinking, (if they are thinking at all), about something else'. This of course is wrong, for if the bracketed words were omitted, the sentence would run on without any stop at all, and the brackets themselves act as their own commas, so to speak. In (iii) on the other hand there would be a comma between 'Corner' and 'where' even if the parenthesis (which belongs, strictly speaking, to the first clause) were omitted; therefore the comma still stands after the closing bracket of the parenthesis. The rule is that a parenthesis should be slipped into the part of the sentence to which it belongs without disturbing the punctuation of the sentence before its intrusion. You will find, as a corollary of this, that while the *closing bracket* of a parenthesis may quite often be *followed* by another stop, as in (iii) and (v) above, there will seldom be occasion for a stop to *precede* an *opening bracket*. Here, however, is one such:

(vi) On New Year's Eve we were informed that the Turk had been cutting our telephone cables in various places, but we did not feel any alarm. (Looking back at this, I am inclined to regard it as one of the first indications of something far more important than any of us then imagined.)

Though parentheses are usually in the form of phrases, clauses, or short sentences slipped into another sentence, they may occasionally be introduced as complete and independent sentences serving as an afterthought to the main context, as in the example above. In such cases the opening bracket must obviously be immediately preceded by a full-stop.

Note in passing the difference in position of the full-stops at the end of (v) and (vi), the one outside the closing bracket and the other within it. In (v) the full-stop belongs to the main sentence, into which a parenthesis happens to have been inserted at the end; the door must, as it were, be closed on the parenthesis by its final bracket before the sentence itself is closed by its own full-stop. In (vi) the whole of the main sentence, to which the full-stop belongs, is itself bracketed; it must be closed by its own full-stop before the bracket comes to mark the end of the parenthesis. No stops are, in fact, admissible *inside brackets* except such as properly belong to the actual words bracketed. Apart from the full-stop just referred to, the comma after 'this' in (vi) and the exclamation-mark after 'omen' in (iii) provide such instances.

Perhaps just a word should be said about the use of the square, as distinct from the common, form of brackets. They generally denote that the parenthesis is rather more of an intrusion than that for which ordinary brackets are employed, and are most commonly used in quotations to introduce words that do not strictly belong to the quotation but are needed to clarify it. Thus:

To quote the words of Macaulay, 'Why a man should be less fit to exercise those powers [of securing property and maintaining order] because he wears a beard, because he does not eat ham, because he goes to the synagogue on Saturdays instead of going to the church on Sundays, we cannot conceive.'

Another example is provided by the second extract in the section on The Dash below: Badcock's name, which did not appear in the actual quotation but in the words immediately preceding it, has been inserted to show who is meant by 'that player'.

THE DASH is a stop which I approach with some trepidation. There are those who refuse to recognize it as a legitimate stop and will have nothing to do with it; yet in some quarters, notably the leading articles of our best newspapers, you may count dashes by the daily dozen. Personally I continually feel the need to make use of them, whilst continually feeling moved to criticize others for overdoing them. I shall therefore have to tread warily. Here are some instances of what appear to me perfectly legitimate and entirely appropriate uses of this stop:

(i) There is nothing to provoke fresh anxiety – rather the reverse – in the news that the Prime Minister has returned to London.

(ii) The Australians would have been struggling desperately had Leyland at mid-on held on to a catch – he seemed certain to after he had knocked the ball up – when that player [Badcock] had made 15.

(iii) Mrs Garon, who had holed everything, putted first and missed. Miss Corlett – hide your heads and weep, ye nymphs of St Anne's – missed too.

(iv) New Zealand electors will be called upon tomorrow to pass judgement upon the Government – the first Labour Government in the Dominion – which they placed in power with a sweeping majority three years ago.

(v) With the exception of the overdrafts of the Primary Products Marketing Department – an exception which is well understood – all advances made by the Bank to the Government have been repaid within the financial year.

(vi) Whether or not J. Borotra wins his ninth championship at Queen's tomorrow – and who would say that he will not? – he enriched our store of memories of a great player yesterday, when he beat C. M. Jones.

(vii) The effort to reduce expenditure by this means has not been a pronounced success – some might count it a complete failure; so some fresh means must be devised.

(viii) The Soviet leaders were in a position to inflict incalculable damage on Britain – at a risk. They have deliberately preferred to offer a compromise – at a price.

(ix) Intellect, industry, integrity, resolute courage, wide sympathy – all the attributes of a noble character were to be found in him to a marked degree.

The most normal use of the dash, or rather a pair of dashes, as may be seen from the first six examples given, closely resembles that of brackets, which could easily be substituted for the former in each of these sentences. If any distinction in usage is to be found, it lies perhaps in an extra touch of abruptness provided by the dash; and, again, if a word out of a preceding clause is, as it

were, picked up afresh and repeated with some added
comment, as in (iv) and (v), dashes are more often used
than brackets (see also pp. 26–7).

The combination of other stops with dashes is even
less admissible than with brackets. No stop should ever
be placed immediately before a dash except a question
mark, as in (vi), or an exclamation mark – in (iii) the
writer might have put one after 'St Anne's'; and no stop
at all can ever come immediately after a dash. A 'closing
dash' (if one may so call it), unlike a closing bracket,
drops out if it comes up against some other stop required
by the main sentence, as in (vii); and from this arises
an independent use of the single dash, from which the
bracket-effect disappears. It may thus be appropriately
used before any afterthought or interjection tacked
on to the end of a sentence, as in (viii); and it is also very
commonly found before a clause that summarizes, or
gathers up the threads of, a list of items or series of clauses
preceding. This use of the dash, approximating to that
of the colon, is illustrated in (ix) above and has also been
noticed on pp. 29 and 41.

Thus the dash is a handy stop for use, either in pairs
or singly, with somewhat abrupt interjections or
'asides' sandwiched into, or tacked on to, a main
sentence. But there are signs that its use is being exten-
ded in such a way as to usurp the function of other stops.
Here are a few instances culled at random from period-
icals of good standing:

(i) The annual rally of the Nazis – in the immense theatres,
arenas, and parade grounds created by their party at
Nuremberg – opens tomorrow.

(ii) A lobbed centre deceived Dawson – who was facing a tearful sun, lately emerged – and the ball struck the crossbar.

(iii) You are one of the few now surviving who are aware of my close association with the late Cecil Rhodes – so the following may be of interest to you and your readers.

(iv) As Captain Dugdale – the skilful translator of these letters – points out, . . .

In (i) no stops at all are needed where the dashes occur; if there must be any, they should be commas. In (ii) commas rather than dashes should appropriately enclose an ordinary non-defining relative clause. In (iii) the dash is uncalled-for; comma, or possibly semi-colon, would be better. In (iv) a simple descriptive phrase in apposition to a proper name should by all the rules be placed between commas. The dash seems often to be the resort of the writer who is either too hurried or too bored to think out which stop is appropriate to his context. No wonder that in some quarters it has fallen into disrepute; but I still maintain that, if kept in its place – and I make one here for it for luck, it is a very useful stop.*

* I have been taken to task by several correspondents, and even in print (by the late G. H. Vallins in his admirable *Better English*), for having in this sentence sinfully failed, or at best inadvertently forgotten, to mark with a dash the end of a parenthesis that opened with one. On the contrary my deliberate purpose was, and is, to illustrate my contention (see p. 73) – the obvious fact, rather – that dashes, unlike brackets, do *not* necessarily work in pairs. Here, without the parenthesis, I should punctuate: 'I still maintain that, if kept in its place, it is a very useful stop'; hence 'I still maintain' that the closing dash must give way to the comma required to mark the deferred close of the 'if' clause at 'luck', just as it gives way to full-stops and semi-colons (see the last three examples on p. 72).

4

A MIXED BAG

Exclamation and Question Marks
Inverted Commas – Hyphens
Capitals – Italics – Paragraphs

OF the EXCLAMATION MARK there is little to be said except that its use should be confined to genuine exclamations: 'Heavens above!', 'Hi, you! Come off the grass!', 'What a shame!', 'How lovely you're looking!' etc. Occasionally a sentence that has the form of an ordinary statement will bear an exclamation mark when the sense demands: e.g. 'He actually climbed up on to the dizzy parapet and balanced himself on one foot!'; 'I *am* surprised to find you here!'. But the merely gushing exclamation mark – 'When we got home, we found the most lovely tea awaiting us, with hot buttered toast, scones, and lots of Devonshire cream!', or 'I'm sure you would adore my new puppy; he has lovely ears and the sweetest little tail!' – is to be avoided; and the doubling, or even trebling, of exclamation marks for the sake of extra emphasis is a vulgarism. Still, these risks do not excuse their omission, not infrequent nowadays with 'What' and 'How' exclamations in particular, sometimes to the detriment of the sense.

QUESTION MARKS likewise can be disposed of quite shortly. They too have their own vulgarism, an attempt to attribute sarcasm to a word by putting a query in brackets after it: 'We attended a really cultured (?) dinner-party last night, at which the other guests could talk of nothing but film stars and football pools.' This habit should be strangled at birth. The only tolerable way of producing the desired effect, if it is not self-evident, is to enclose the ironical word in inverted commas.

There is, however, one other misuse of the question mark that deserves more serious comment, namely its intrusion in *indirect* questions, such as:

He asked me why I was so silent?

This is definitely wrong. The original question mark of 'Why are you so silent?' must give way to a full-stop when the question is converted by 'He asked me' into its indirect form, for the sentence *as a whole* has now become a statement.

Nevertheless there are occasions on which a sentence which is not actually in the form of a question may be followed by a question mark. It is possible, when speaking, for the tone of the voice to turn what is a statement in form into a question in effect, and a question mark is naturally required to reproduce this on paper. Thus:

Surely you will not attempt to play in such abominable weather as this?

You're back already? You have not been to the theatre, then?

[On this and the next section see also pp. 115-17.]

INVERTED COMMAS need cause little trouble if it is

remembered that, so far as their main function of denoting direct speech is concerned, they must enclose the *actual* words of the speaker, and not any version of them that is in the slightest degree indirect. This may seem a very elementary rule, but it is one that is not invariably observed. Here is a not uncommon type of the breach of it:

I was proud when he referred to me as 'one of his young men'.

'One of his young men' were *not* his actual words, but 'one of my young men'; so either 'his' must be altered to 'my' or the inverted commas must go. And the following instance is doubly at fault:

He respectfully asked 'if she was in the same mind as yesterday?'

Either the words within quotes must become 'Are you in . . . yesterday?' (note the capital) or both quotes and question mark (see p. 76, middle) must be dropped.

Similarly in reported speech it is not unusual to find this sort of thing:

He said that 'it was a mistake to attach all the blame to one side. Both parties have grievances, which need to be handled impartially and sympathetically. . . .'

He did not say 'it *was* a mistake' but 'it *is* a mistake'. The literal words of the speaker do not, therefore, begin until after 'was'. If we want the inverted commas to come immediately after the verb of saying, we must change the tense of 'was', drop the 'that' and write:

He said, 'It is a mistake. . . .'

Otherwise the inverted commas must be deferred until the speaker's actual words begin:

He said that it was 'a mistake to attach all the blame . . .'.

Actually, if the latter alternative were adopted, it would be rather more natural to defer the inverted commas still further, especially as the word 'have' in the second sentence is the first infallible sign that direct speech has started. Thus:

He said that it was a mistake to attach all the blame to one side. 'Both parties have grievances. . . .'

Having got this point firmly established, we can turn to the association of inverted commas with other stops. It is customary to insert a comma after a simple verb of saying, asking etc. that immediately precedes a sentence in inverted commas, and likewise a comma after the final word enclosed in inverted commas when the verb of saying etc. immediately follows.

He replied, 'I have no idea what you are talking about.'

'I have no idea what you are talking about,' he replied.

'I have no idea', he replied, 'what you are talking about.'

But note what happens to a sentence divided into two clauses by a heavier stop with a verb of saying interposed.

I have no idea what you are talking about; perhaps you will explain.

becomes

'I have no idea what you are talking about', he replied; 'perhaps you will explain.'

You may want to keep the semi-colon in its original position after 'about' in spite of the insertion of 'he replied', because it seems to belong to 'about' in the original sentence. But in normal usage 'he replied', with its preceding comma, squeezes its way in before the semi-colon.

On the position of stops in relation to 'closing quotes' I am deliberately silent, as this is usually subject to the House Rules of individual printing firms (and contentious at that).

If a passage in inverted commas is prefaced by something more formal or elaborate than a plain verb of saying etc., a colon may take the place of a comma. Thus:

The General sent for the officers and addressed them in these words: 'Gentlemen, you have been called upon to undertake a very difficult and dangerous task. . . .'

But the growing habit of invariably prefacing quotes by colons, whatever the prefacing verb and however brief the remark following, seems needlessly fussy. In such sentences as the following I would replace the colons by commas – or preferably no stop at all:

The General said: 'Good morning, gentlemen.'

If you said: 'White' to him he would certainly say: 'Black', but if you asked him his honest opinion he was very likely to consider carefully and reply: 'Grey'.

There is no technical distinction between single and double inverted commas. It is obviously convenient to have two kinds when the necessity arises of using one set within another, e.g.

'Messiou,' said the colonel, exasperated, 'I am going to play "Destiny Waltz" for you.'

'After the war,' said General Bramble, 'if I am still alive, I shall have a stone carved with "Here lies a soldier and a sportsman".'

In general it is a matter of choice; but with titles – The 'Casse-Noisette' Suite, 'The Goat and Compasses', the 'Roaring Forties' – single quotes are rather more often used.

HYPHENS, or rather the omission of them, can be the cause of more trouble than might at first be supposed. Pairs of words apt to be used in close association go through three stages of evolution. Starting as separate words, in the course of a growing attachment they become hyphened, until eventually the hyphen drops out and the two words become one. Such words as 'landlord', 'playmate', 'boatman', 'handkerchief', 'waistcoat', with scores of others, have reached the final stage; whilst 'wash-basin', 'wrist-watch', 'tie-pin', 'scrap-book', 'india-rubber' etc. are still at the halfway stage.

I need not elaborate this point, which can be found treated much more adequately in books more learned than this. We are concerned here with punctuation, not with the evolution of language. Yet we cannot afford to lose sight of the latter when engaged on the simple task of putting in or leaving out hyphens, for we have to judge in each case what stage of evolution our pairs of words have reached. This we can decide only by observation and instinct, and even so there will be plenty of room for difference of opinion, for while some words have firmly established themselves on one side or other of the fence, others are still sitting on it. A time will presumably come when 'break-neck' and 'lift-man' will look every bit as odd as 'break-fast' and 'sports-man' would look today, but the two former have settled down pretty comfortably in the hyphened stage for the time being, while the two latter have long since qualified for the one-word stage. On the other hand words like 'hat-box', 'pipe-clay', 'good-night', 'hand-shake' are still wobbling between the hyphen and the one-word stage, whilst others like 'coal mine', 'tobacco pouch', 'blotting pad', 'waste paper' are not yet in undisputed possession of their hyphens. A few words seem to be condemned to float perpetually between all three stages, e.g. 'common sense', 'common-sense', and 'commonsense'; and 'good will' similarly.

What we decide to do about hyphens in these compound words does not matter very much so long as we use a reasonable amount of common sense (or common-sense?). But there is one other point besides their stage of evolution that, I think, should be borne in mind, namely the appearance which they are going to assume when the hyphen drops out. I will give only one instance. If anything be needed to denote the specialized sense of the words 'public house', most people would, I imagine, be content with 'public-house'. It used to be printed 'publichouse' in *The Times* (they seem now to have thought better of it); and I for one can never read this horrid word without wanting to run the 'ch' together, as in 'artichoke'. If the compounding of two words into one is going to have an effect that is displeasing or confusing to the eye, I submit that they should be left hyphened for good and all.

From confusion of sight or sound let us proceed to confusion of sense, in which connection also the hyphen has a part to play. When two words which do not normally need a hyphen are used in combination as a single epithet, they should be hyphened; for instance, 'the poets of the nineteenth century' becomes 'the nineteenth-century poets'. In this particular case no confusion would arise from failure to observe this rule; but the description (often to be found in the press) of a cricket match as 'a low scoring game', instead of 'a low-scoring game', sounds hardly complimentary. The argument that the two epithets are obviously meant to be compounded because they are not separated by a comma is not good enough, for, as I have pointed out on p. 63, the insertion of such commas is not invariable. The fact remains that the omission of a hyphen *may* result in ambiguity (or absurdity), and indeed quite frequently does. Here are a few instances, and more are noticed in Chapter 7 (p. 119).

(i) He hit one shoulder high past Benaud.

(ii) The atmosphere was very like that of many European villages I have visited in little frequented places.

(iii) The clergy of the Church of England included the hardest working men in the land.

(iv) She was regularly present at the end of term parties.

(v) The first air dropped hydrogen bomb. . . .

(vi) They emphasized that the horse had advantages for a break through which the foot had not.

I am not going to pretend that all of these are equally ambiguous. The reader may not take more than a second to correct his fleeting impression that (i) the batsman's shoulder was sent skimming over Benaud's head, that (iii) the Church of England has more than its fair quota of clerical 'toughs', that (iv) the lady was either unpunctual or unlucky, or that (v) it was the air that dropped the bomb. But to be led even for one second 'up the garden path', when reading, is tiresome; and anyway sentences like (ii) and (vi) may cause more than a moment's confusion and delay. 'Little frequented places' means almost exactly the opposite of 'little-frequented places'; and I took some little time puzzling over the 'break', in (vi), 'through which the foot' were somehow frustrated, before I realized that the writer was talking about a 'break-through'.

A few other hyphen problems, on which views may differ, are mentioned in Chapter 7, pp. 118–19; but one form of omission of the hyphen, with words that are pure prefixes though not actually coalescing with the word that follows them, is inexcusable. Most people would think twice before writing 'Ex President', but many are quite prepared to write 'Vice Chancellor'; yet both are on exactly the same footing and in both the hyphen is equally essential.

I have now dealt with all the stops except the Apostrophe, which I mention merely in order that it may not feel neglected. It seems hardly necessary to state that it precedes the 's' of the possessive case in singular words (and plurals that do not end in 's') and follows it in plurals that end in 's' ('at his mother's knee', 'The

Women's Institute', 'The Mothers' Union'); that to denote the possessive of singular words that already end in 's' it may either stand alone after that 's' or precede an extra one (St Thomas' or St Thomas's); and that with the possessive pronouns 'hers', 'yours', 'theirs', and 'its' it drops out altogether. Having said that much – and I had almost forgotten to mention that it is also used to indicate the omission of a letter ('don't' for 'do not' etc.) – I feel that I have done my duty by the apostrophe. Would that all stops gave so little trouble!

The remaining sections of this chapter, though not concerned with actual stops, seem to me to fit in better here than anywhere else.

CAPITALS. – I have often heard people say 'I wish someone would tell me the rules about the use of capital letters'. My answer would be, 'There are no rules – or at all events precious few – about the use of capital letters. The main thing is to be consistent.' There is of course one rule, that capitals should be used for all proper names; and I myself would reckon as equivalent to a rule the practice of giving an initial capital to a word other than a proper noun (except 'and', 'of', 'in' etc.) whenever it forms part of a title. The learned editors of *The Cambridge History of English Literature* followed a peculiar method in this respect, eschewing capital letters in many titles, such as 'bishop of Chester', 'provost of Trinity college, Dublin', 'the court of Star chamber', 'lord Macaulay' etc.; yet they did not go to the logical length of writing 'sir Walter Scott', 'the merchant of Venice', and so forth, nor, I imagine, would they have cared to see their work referred to as 'the Cambridge history of English literature'. This sort of thing seems to me to savour of crankiness. It is a well-established convention that initial capitals should be used in all formal titles, whether of books, plays, ranks, appointments, public bodies, public-houses, or patent medicines; and the line of distinction between the general and the titular use of a word is a perfectly easy one to draw. One speaks of 'bishops, priests, and deacons' but of 'the Bishop of Chichester'; of 'university professors' but of 'the Professor of Poetry at Oxford University'; of 'transport companies' but of 'the Shell Transport Company'; of 'a brigade of infantry' but of 'the 18th Infantry Brigade'.

There remain certain words that even in their general use are often, but not always, given initial capitals. Such words as 'army', 'navy', 'colonel', 'bank holiday', 'rugby' (applied to football), 'committee', 'republic' occur to me at random, but most readers will probably have their own list of bogies – for the problem whether to use capitals or not for such words seems really to worry some people. I see no reason why it should. After all, what does it matter whether we write 'He was summoned before the committee' or 'He was summoned before the Committee'; 'I received a message from the colonel' or 'I received a message from the Colonel'? In the case of 'He was summoned before the Committee of Privileges' or 'I received a message from Colonel Blimp' there is only one proper course to adopt, but in the other cases I submit that there is no right or wrong way. To give any ruling on such uses is neither possible nor desirable. The writer should follow his own bent, only taking care to be consistent within the limits of any one book, article, or other form of composition on which he is engaged. In a book relating to the Civil War which I read the other day there were numerous references to 'the Army' throughout the first 300 pages and to 'the army' in the last hundred. Possibly a good many readers would never notice the inconsistency, but there is something to be said for being orderly and methodical even in minor points of detail.

There are a few words normally requiring an initial capital that, when applied to common objects, exchange the capital for a small letter. Most of them are place-names (or adjectives formed therefrom) that have in course of time lost their purely local association. I have in mind 'india-rubber', 'brussels sprouts', 'roman type', 'french windows', 'venetian blinds'; and readers will no doubt be able to supply plenty of others.

Need I mention the necessity of using a capital letter not merely immediately after a full-stop, but even after a comma when the latter precedes the opening words of a quotation or direct speech in inverted commas (e.g. 'He replied, "It is no business of yours"'); or the custom in poetry of starting each fresh line with a capital, irrespective of the stop (if any) at the end of the preceding line? I hardly think so, but at any rate I've done it now. [See also Chapter 7, pp. 119–21.]

The most common uses of ITALICS are:

I. To pick out words for special emphasis. Thus used, italics are equivalent in printing to underlining in manuscript. They are useful for denoting in the written word shades of expression that the speaker would make clear by the tone of his voice; also, apart from any considerations of voice, for making words stand out boldly to the eye.

He *is* a villainous-looking scoundrel.

It is no good telling me that the papers *were* in the safe.

The main thing is that the country should do something about it and *do it now*.

This is a practice, however, which should be used only when the required emphasis could not be 'got across' otherwise, which is comparatively seldom. Too liberal use of italics, as of exclamation marks, becomes gushing and tiresome, and is liable to defeat its own object.

II. To pick out foreign words introduced singly or in short phrases into an English sentence (for longer passages inverted commas are more ordinarily used).

Without being particularly intelligent, he had plenty of *savoir faire*.

It is possible to make out a *prima facie* case against this policy, but it would be a mistake to reject it *in toto*.

III. To pick out the titles of books, newspapers, plays etc.

The *French Revolution* was followed by *Lectures on Heroes and Hero-worship*, which contain the fullest statement of Carlyle's attitude towards history.

Inverted commas are an alternative now seldom preferred, though commonly used for the titles of individual songs, poems, journal articles etc. (It is perhaps worth observing that in the last example *The French Revolution* is strictly the form in which those words should be printed if the precise title of Carlyle's work is not 'French Revolution' but 'The French Revolution', as in fact appears on the title-page of my own copy. I have, however, reproduced the sentence exactly as it is printed in *The Cambridge History of English Literature*.)

PARAGRAPHS. – This judicious division of subject-matter into paragraphs is a task on which author or editor needs to spend some care, for it affects the 'readability' as well as the sense of what is written. It is natural that a writer should start a fresh paragraph whenever he enters on a new topic, or on a fresh stage in his topic, for this will help the reader to keep as it were in step with the author. But the mere appearance of the reading-matter has an effect too, if only subconscious, on the reader. Pages of letterpress divided into paragraphs at fairly frequent intervals are more inviting to the eye than those that run on with never a paragraph from top to bottom. I say *fairly* frequent intervals, however, with intent, for a pointless profusion of paragraphs seems to me as irritating as their absence is forbidding. The cheaper journalism has adopted in some quarters the fashion of starting a fresh paragraph with almost every new sentence. Let me give one or two instances:

(i) After the Suez Canal, Haifa represented the greatest commitment of the British Fleet in the Mediterranean.

This was because the pipe line which brings oil – that sinew of modern war and industry – 1,000-odd miles across the desert from Kirkuk has one of its two Mediterranean terminals at Haifa.

The pipe line had only been opened in January 1935.

When the emergency arose in the Eastern Mediterranean Haifa was quite undefended.

There was no harbour capable of accommodating large numbers of warships, or of being closed by a defensive boom.

For this reason its defence presented a problem widely different from that at Alexandria.

(ii) In any case, let me remind you, Christianity is not so much a way of living as a motive for living. That is where nine people out of ten go wrong.

The New Testament certainly describes a way of living.

It speaks about great moral principles which, as I believe, are eternal in the universe.

Man did not make those principles; neither can he destroy them. It is not we who break the Ten Commandments.

They break us. Surely we have lived long enough to discover that. But that is not the end of it.

Those moral principles in the New Testament are linked always to a Personality. The motive of them is to be always love and loyalty to that Personality.

Likewise the power to make them work in practical life is said to come not from within ourselves only, but from that same Personality.

(iii) Their expenses are heavy, however, and the strain of riding exacts a spartan life.

For they are at it throughout the year. In the winter they ride in Australia.

(iv) While I was there Deauville enjoyed its biggest night's profit of the season – 2,000,000 francs, about £12,000.

Reduced to £3,000 by the time the Government have taken 65 per cent and the town 10 per cent!

The first of these extracts should be divided into two paragraphs at most, the second beginning at 'When the emergency arose . . .'. The sense is all against starting fresh paragraphs at any of the other four places so treated. The last two examples are included merely in order to show the lengths to which this sort of thing can go nowadays; in each case a new paragraph actually starts in the middle of a sentence wrongly broken by a full-stop.

The disfigurement of the second passage, which is by a serious and cultured writer, must surely be due not to him, but to some miscreant in the editorial department. It deserves to be analysed a little more carefully than the others. It has more than twice as many paragraphs as the sense admits, including two at points where the start of a new paragraph is particularly jarring – 'It speaks about . . .' and 'They break us'. On the other hand one point where a new paragraph is just possible ('But that is not . . .') is passed over in favour of a less suitable point a sentence later. Allowing for a fresh paragraph wherever there is the slightest pretext for one, I would rearrange the passage as follows, and I suggest that this form restores to it some of the dignity of which the other has robbed it, besides making the thread of the argument clearer:

In any case, let me remind you, Christianity is not so much a way of living as a motive for living. That is where nine people out of ten go wrong.

The New Testament certainly describes a way of living. It speaks about great moral principles which, as I believe, are eternal in the universe. Man did not make those principles; neither can he destroy them. It is not we who break the Ten Commandments. They break us. Surely we have lived long enough to discover that.

But that is not the end of it. Those moral principles in the New Testament are linked always to a Personality. The motive of them is to be always love and loyalty to that Personality. Likewise the power to make them work in practical life is said to come not from within ourselves only, but from that same Personality.

This abominable habit of cutting up English periods into contemptible little snippets of a dozen or so words apiece is presumably due to the notion that that is the only form in which the reading public can be induced to absorb articles of any length. It is a pity that editors should rate the intelligence of their readers so low, but the real menace of it is that if this kind of thing is ladled out to the man in the street for long enough he may in the course of time really become incapable of digesting anything more solid. It would seem to me better to reduce paragraphs to a bare minimum than to sprinkle them all over the page without rhyme or reason in this shoddy fashion; but the soundest policy, of course, is to aim at a happy mean.

I need hardly add that nothing which I have said has any bearing on the arrangement of conversational passages, in which it has long been customary to start a fresh line with each speaker, however 'snippety' the result may be.

SOME COMMON PITFALLS

In this chapter I propose to deal with some of the minor errors of grammar and style that are most often in evidence today. It has no claim to be in any way comprehensive. The reader who expects light to be shed on each and every problem that may cause him doubt or difficulty has only to consult Fowler's *Modern English Usage*, where he can be sure of finding the matter treated fully, authoritatively, and indeed humorously. The particular points which I have selected are, as I have said, those which seem to me to crop up most frequently; and they are all, moreover, the type of mistake that editor or proof-reader can put right by some quite simple alteration that should not offend the susceptibility of the writer – if he notices it at all.

PARTICIPLES are among the commonest sources of error nowadays. One or two privileged participles, such as 'considering', 'owing to', have by centuries of usage earned the right to be used 'absolutely', i.e. without needing to be attached to some neighbouring noun. Here is an example:

Considering all the circumstances, the decision seems a very reasonable one.

In accordance with strict grammar 'considering' should agree with 'the decision', with the nonsensical result that it is the decision itself that is considering all the circumstances. But the idea underlying the words is '[To us] considering all the circumstances, the decision seems a very reasonable one', and this particular usage has long since become well established and clearly understood.

These few exceptions apart, it should be remembered that a participle *must* agree with some noun in the sentence in which it occurs, and when there is more than one noun, that which comes nearest to the participle is usually the one to which the participle will most naturally be attached. Writers often fall into the mistake of making a participle apparently refer to the noun to which in sense it does not refer, and in such cases all that is needed is a slight alteration in the position of the participial clause. For instance, in this sentence:

Instead of rowing the full-course trial, Mr C. W. Wise, who was in charge, set the crew to row from Barnes Bridge to Hammersmith Bridge.

it would appear that Mr Wise, bursting with energy, originally contemplated rowing the full-course trial himself. Alter the order thus:

Mr C. W. Wise, who was in charge, set the crew, instead of rowing the full-course trial, to row from . . . etc.

and not only does the writer's meaning immediately become plain, but the sentence also becomes strictly grammatical.

No less common is the even worse mistake of using a participle in such a way that, when attached to the *only* noun with which it can grammatically agree, the result is sheer nonsense, as in the following:

Yesterday from my windows, gazing down on to the traffic, a horse cart plodded, as only horse carts will, along the busy street.

At the risk of being very unpopular with my readers, I should like to make a suggestion to you regarding Variety.
Coming from me, probably no one will be more surprised than yourself.

In the first of these examples the only thing that, grammatically, could have been gazing down 'from my windows' was the horse cart, which, oddly enough, was at the same time plodding along the busy street! In the second (note with disgust, incidentally, the new paragraph at 'Coming') what is 'coming from me' must either be 'no one' or just possibly 'yourself'; the participle has got to be attached to one or other, almost inevitably the former. If writers would only give a moment's thought to the noun to which their participle really refers and then *make sure to bring it into the sentence as soon as possible*, this violation of both sense and grammar would be avoided. In the first of the above examples, for instance, the writer has only to say:

Yesterday from my windows, gazing down on to the traffic, *I saw* a horse cart plodding . . .

and he has done the trick. The second example will need just a little more alteration, but the early insertion after the participle of the noun ('suggestion' from the previous sentence) to which that participle must refer will produce the solution quite readily:

Coming from me, *this suggestion* will probably surprise no one more than yourself.

Though by now I have probably made my point clear enough, I cannot resist quoting one really prize effort as a further illustration of it. It is an extract from a short article contributed a few years ago to a leading newspaper by 'A Correspondent'.

Yesterday all former feats were eclipsed by a Keswick mountaineer, Mr Robert Graham. The performance must now rank as the world's mountain walking record. Acting on the advice of Mr G. D. Abraham the well-known rock climber, the route over the highest Peaks of the Lake District was taken in the reverse direction to that usually followed.

Starting from Keswick Town Hall at 1 o'clock on Sunday morning Skiddaw was climbed by the ordinary route. Then, descending into Skiddaw Forest, Great Calva was surmounted on the way over Saddleback, whence the descent was made to Threlkeld and so up to Wanthwaite Pike, to begin the long, long stretch over the various Dodds of Helvellyn. . . . Oncoming darkness made the final section trying, but, paced by Mr Hewitson, Dale Head was climbed, and by Hindscarth, Robinson, and High Snab, the Vale of Newlands was finally gained near Mill Dam Inn at eight minutes short of midnight.

From this extract may be noticed another of the causes that lead to trouble with participles, namely the peculiar aversion shown by some writers to the use of active verbs. All would have been plain sailing (or rather, climbing) if the writer of the above had not been so passionately wedded to the passive voice – 'Acting on the advice of . . . Mr Graham took the route over . . . Starting from Keswick . . . he climbed Skiddaw . . . Then descending . . . he surmounted Great Calva . . .'

and so on. As it is, the route over the highest Peaks of the Lake District apparently condescended to act on Mr Abraham's advice, to begin with. But this is a prelude to still stranger happenings. Skiddaw decides to start from Keswick Town Hall in the small hours of a Sunday morning, after which Great Calva is found descending into Skiddaw Forest; and finally Dale Head, not to be out of the running, goes so far as to secure the services of Mr Hewitson as pacer. Talk of moving mountains!

'FOLLOWING.' – The misuse of this participle in particular has become so general and so flagrant that it demands a short section to itself. All those who have any respect for the English language should be grateful to Sir Alan Herbert for his crusade against the atrocities daily committed with this word. So far as I am aware, he has till now conducted it single-handed, but I propose to enlist my puny forces, for what they are worth, under his standard.

As I pointed out at the beginning of the last section, a very limited number of participles, such as 'considering', have succeeded in establishing their right to be used absolutely, and the 'following' fanatics may argue – if they have troubled to think out their position at all – that 'following' stands in the same category. It does not. To begin with, it cannot boast the long pedigree of 'considering'. The cheaper journalism decided, as it were, overnight that it was entitled to be used absolutely, and within a comparatively few years that use has spread to those who ought to know better. More important than that, 'considering' no doubt owes its privileged position to the fact that the only substitutes for it are such rather awkward phrases as 'in view of', 'with regard to'. For 'following', on the other hand, there is, in the use to which I refer, a perfectly good substitute, the simple preposition 'after'. What the luckless 'after' has done to merit being quietly cold-shouldered out of the language I cannot conceive. Many writers of today seem to regard it as unclean, and in the effort to avoid using it they indulge in such idiocies as these:

Following dinner, the band of the Guards played a selection of music in the blue drawing-room.

One hopes that the band managed to overtake their dinner before the evening was out.

Following a chase half across Europe, a beautiful spy was captured at Bucharest.

The lady was apparently following the chase that was following her. It sounds like a vicious circle.

Following a scrummage near the 'twenty-five', the forwards rushed the ball over their opponents' goal-line and another try resulted.

What business had the forwards to be following the scrummage? They ought to have been in it. Try or no try, they should be booted out of the side.

It is of course possible to use an occasional 'following' both grammatically and sensibly in contexts of this type. There is nothing wrong, for instance, with:

Following an attack of influenza, pneumonia set in and the patient became seriously ill.

Here 'following' can and does agree grammatically

with 'pneumonia' and pneumonia can, and in this case
did, follow influenza. Even so, 'after' would have been
both shorter and simpler. Poor old 'after'! I am afraid
that we have nearly seen the last of him, unless Sir
Alan and I can do something about it.

'DUE TO.' – Confusion of a somewhat similar kind is
becoming increasingly common with the phrase 'due
to', which many writers imagine that they can use as a
substitute for 'owing to' as often as they like. Now
'owing to' is, as already noted, one of those few
participles that can be used absolutely. We can say with
impunity 'Owing to a severe illness he was obliged to
cancel all his engagements', although there is no one
word in the sentence to which 'owing' can be sensibly
attached. Grammatically it should be attached to 'he',
but that would not make sense; actually it qualifies the
whole statement that he was obliged to cancel all his
engagements. This use of 'owing to' has established
itself as grammatical simply because there is no better
short way of expressing the meaning required. But
'due' is an adjective and must be capable of attachment
to some one word or phrase in its sentence. If 'due to'
were substituted for 'owing to' in the above sentence,
it would have to qualify 'he' and would thus be wrong,
as it is in the following:

(i) We went on the court at 7 o'clock, due to a long series
of matches preceding ours.

(ii) Largely due to the defence efforts of the western
Powers, Europe was in a state of stalemate.

In (i) neither 'we' nor 'the court' nor '7 o'clock', but

'[the fact that] we went on the court at 7 o'clock' was 'due to a long series of matches preceding ours'. In (ii) what was 'due to the defence efforts ...' was not 'Europe', but, again, '[the fact that] Europe was in a state of stalemate.' In order to make the sentences grammatical, 'due to' must be replaced by 'owing to' or 'because of' – or, indeed, in the second example (from a *Times* leader, alas!) simply 'through'. Here, on the other hand, is an instance of 'due to' used quite legitimately:

There was a real and growing sense of anxiety due to fears that we were not going to be in a position, because of anything which had been produced up to now, to fulfil the Baldwin pledge.

What was due to the 'fears'? Simply and solely the 'sense of anxiety', with which 'due' can and does agree.

MISFITS. – I cannot think of any other title for the error to which I now want to refer, nor of any clear and concise definition of it. I had better illustrate it without further ado.

(i) He can, and often has, changed the course of a game in a few overs.

(ii) The setting up of the Republic has not, and could not, affect the dependence of Ireland on the British market.

(iii) We have not nor shall we ever advocate this policy.

The fault lies in combining with two auxiliaries a part of the main verb which will not fit both of them. Hence in (i), (ii), the writers have in fact said 'can changed', 'has not affect' (the bracket-commas round the intervening words expose this all the more clearly); and in (iii) 'we have not advocate'. Grammar demands in these cases that brevity be sacrificed and the verb be properly completed each time – 'He can change and often has changed . . .', '. . . has not affected and could not affect . . .', 'We have not advocated nor shall we ever advocate . . .'.

Expressions of comparison are especially apt to lead the unwary into this pitfall. In

In the tight scrummages the University forwards got the ball quite as frequently if not more frequently than their opponents . . .

the writer has actually, though inadvertently, said 'as frequently . . . than'. The proper form of the expression of course is: '. . . quite as frequently as, if not more frequently than, their opponents', and the commas are a helpful addition.

'IMPRACTICAL', common in U.S.A., is steadily pushing its way into our highest literary circles. Less mildly disapproving than Fowler, I dare to call it a meaningless mongrel that should be put in permanent quarantine. There is a clear distinction in meaning between 'practical' and 'practicable'. Their negative forms are 'unpractical' and 'impracticable' respectively. When I read (again in a *Times* leader) about 'resolutions that are impractical', I don't know whether this signifies that they are impossible, or merely cumbersome, to carry out. So wherever this wretched word occurs I'm left wondering what the dickens the writer *means*.

DUPLICATED 'THAT'. In indirect statements, especially rather lengthy ones, the word 'that' is liable to be repeated redundantly. This sometimes occurs, too, in quite short sentences, e.g.

You cannot say that on your review of all the evidence in this case that on any day or week he made up his mind to kill his patient?

and in a letter to *The Times* signed by three Peers:

We believe that on the contrary that the Admiralty is thinking ahead on sound and imaginative lines.

RELATIVE CLAUSES AND THEIR COUPLINGS present some tricky problems, on which those who have the leisure should consult *Modern English Usage* (pp. 717 ff.). Those who have not will do well to use such couplings as 'and who [which]' only when preceded by another relative, or quasi-relative, clause. Thus:

The authorities who are most often consulted and who can be generally relied on . . .

The authorities most often consulted and who can be generally relied on . . .

are both legitimate. But it is apparently all too easy to step over the borderline into such faulty expressions as:

(i) In other departments, a tribute must be paid to the excellent and sustained fielding of England, and which was superior to that of Australia.

(ii) X, the possessor of a most effective backhand and who took service notably well in the backhand court . . .

(iii) I came forward as the opponent of the party in power, and which I described in my address as 'a rapacious, tyrannical, and incapable faction'.

In all these three the 'ands' preceding the relatives are unnecessary, and indeed ungrammatical.

'DIFFERENT TO', 'CENTRE ROUND'. – The fact that people and things cannot 'differ to' one another strikes me as sufficient justification (*pace* Fowler) for preferring 'different from' to 'different to'; and even though 'to' has been, and still is, so used by many good writers, I still cannot regard its correction to 'from' as 'mere pedantry'. Similarly (though here there is no guidance in *Modern English Usage*) the even more common 'centre round' seems to me to be bad English: a thing can 'centre in' or 'on'; or it can 'revolve round'. The author who is thus corrected by the printer's reader has cause for gratitude rather than resentment.

'ONLY.' I had intended to say something about the misplacement of 'only', so common nowadays as to have become almost the rule rather than the exception. E.g. when we say 'He only thought of the plan a few days ago', we ought strictly to mean that he *only thought of* it, as distinct from deciding on it, or talking about it, or something of that sort; whereas what we really mean of course is that he thought of it *only a few days*, as opposed to weeks or months, ago. Why not then say 'He thought of it only a few days ago' and have done with it? The author of *Modern English Usage*, however, tells me that it is pedantic to be over-particular about placing 'only' as near as possible to the word which it strictly qualifies unless failure to do so is going to cause real ambiguity. Nine times out of ten it does not, so I will say no more about it.

All the same, I am going to say something about the misplacement of 'not only', when followed by 'but' or 'but also', because not only is it of common occurrence but it does frequently lead to ambiguity (I've done it right on this occasion). Here is an instance of the kind of thing I mean:

This necessitated, not only the resignations of Essex and Manchester, against whom it was chiefly aimed, but also such valuable men as Lord Warwick, who as Lord High Admiral had successfully held the seas for Parliament during those anxious years.

This sentence is illogical. The effect of 'not only ... but also' is precisely the same as that of 'firstly ... secondly' or (i), (ii). Test this sentence by that method (as always, when in doubt about the position of 'not only') and see what you get. Something or other apparently necessitated (i) the resignations of Essex and Manchester; (ii) such valuable men as Lord Warwick. But did it really 'necessitate such valuable men as Lord Warwick'? No; it obviously necessitated the resignations (i) of Essex and Manchester; (ii) of such valuable men as Lord Warwick (or, if you prefer, the resignations of (i) E. and M.; (ii) such valuable men as W.). Accordingly the sentence should read:

This necessitated *the resignations not only of* Essex and Manchester, against whom it was chiefly aimed, but also *of* such valuable men as Lord Warwick, who ... etc.

(If you prefer to put 'not only' after the first 'of', you will not need a second 'of' before 'such'.)

'Not only' could maintain the place it occupies in the original if 'but also' were followed by some such words as 'the dismissal of'. Apply for yourself the test recommended above and you will find that, though of course the sense has been altered, there is nothing amiss with the sentence as such in that form. But wait a moment! As this book is mainly concerned with punctuation, let us have a final dig at the utterly superfluous comma after 'necessitated'.

6

PROOF-CORRECTION[*]

THE task of correcting proofs is not confined to the professional writer and the professional proof-reader; it is the sort of job which at one time or another may fall to the lot of almost anybody, whether it be a concert programme, a school magazine, an examination paper, or a menu that he has to see through the press. Most of us can get along well enough by the light of nature and the use of common sense, but there are certain 'rules of the game' and it is just as well to know them. Time and trouble will then be saved for both ourselves and the printers.

At the end of this chapter are appended two pages, one marked with the author's corrections and the other showing the corrections carried out. Before dealing with these corrections in detail, however, I should like to dispose of one or two general points.

Corrections may be written on both margins of the page. Usually, of course, the margin nearer to the mistake in the text will be found the more convenient, but there is no need to be bound by that consideration if there are others that outweigh it. The inner margin may be so narrow that it will barely take more than a one-letter correction, and in any case it is better to put an

[*This chapter has been slightly revised in accordance with British Standards for proof-correction.]

occasional correction in the margin further from the
error than to get the other margin so congested as to
cause inconvenience to yourself and possibly confusion
to the printer. It is customary to draw an oblique line
on the right-hand side of each marginal correction; this
helps to make an isolated correction catch the printer's
eye, and if there is more than one misprint in the same
line of text the oblique lines help to keep the marginal
corrections separate and distinct. When a corrected
proof is returned to the printer, it should be marked at
the top 'Revise' if the author wishes to see a further
proof after correction, or 'Press' if the author is content to let final printing follow correction without any
further checking on his own part.

Now for the specimen given on p. 112. I will take
each individual correction, working downwards from
the top of the page and reading from left to right.

The deletion of anything in the text which has to go
out, *without being replaced by anything else*, is denoted by
putting a line through whatever requires deletion and
writing a 'delete' sign (see line 1) in the margin.

The omission of anything that requires insertion is
denoted by putting a 'caret-mark' in the text at the
point where the omission occurs and writing the missing
stop, letter, word etc. inthe margin (as lines 1 and 3).
Note that, as the letter missing from the page-heading
is an italic capital, the marginal correction denotes this
precisely; it is just as well to be careful in this matter even
when, as here, the printer would be hardly likely to go
wrong.

When wrong stops or letters in the text have to be
deleted *and replaced by other stops or letters*, put a line

through the offending letter etc. in the text and write the correct one in the margin. That is all that is required. I emphasize this because many people have a notion that a delete sign or a caret-mark should precede the correction in the margin; or, again, that if one or two letters of a word are wrong, the whole word must be crossed out in the text and rewritten in the margin. The third line of the specimen page illustrates the correction of a portion of a word, and in the fourth line there are two words each of which requires the correction of only a single letter.

The next two corrections illustrate transpositions, in the first instance of two letters and in the second of two words. A kind of 'switch-back' line in the text is supplemented by the abbreviation 'trs.' in the margin.

A treble underline denotes large capitals and a double one small capitals; 'c. & s.c.' does perfectly well as a marginal indication, though the fuller form of the abbreviation is 'cap. & sm. caps.'.

The three corrections that follow involve conventional signs. Where an extra space intrudes, as between the two letters of the word 'it' in the 9th line, a kind of double 'slur' is made in the text above and below the gap and is repeated in the margin. Conversely, where a space is omitted, as between 'may' and 'not', a sign resembling the sharp in music is put in the margin, but all that is needed in the text is a perpendicular line through the place where the space is required. The 'squiggle' in the margin denoting an upside-down letter in the following line defies precise description; in the text the offending letter needs merely to be circled.

Two lines lower down, a letter from a different type

has slipped into the word 'plurals'. Again the offending letter should be circled in the text, and the letters 'w.f.' (meaning 'wrong fount') should be written in the margin. The same word is in trouble in the next line, some of its letters being out of alignment. The method of correction is to put a line above and below the misplaced letters in the text and to repeat the double horizontal lines in the margin.

The next correction shows the conversion of a small initial letter into a capital; and immediately below is the reverse process: to give 'Possessive' a small 'p', put a line through the 'P' and write 'l.c.' (meaning 'lower case') in the margin.

To convert a word from italic type into roman, circle it and write 'rom.' in the margin; conversely, to convert it from roman into italics, underline it and write 'ital.' in the margin. This disposes of the next three corrections.

The omission of a stop is, in accordance with the rule already stated, indicated in the text simply by a caret-mark at the appropriate place; but in the matter of marginal correction different stops require slightly different treatment. All stops except hyphen, dash, full-stop, colon, and inverted commas are written in the margin with no addition save the usual oblique line. A hyphen or dash in the margin, however, should have a perpendicular line on each side of it, full-stop and colon should be encircled, inverted commas should be accompanied by the kind of mark shown in the margin opposite the 24th and 25th lines of the specimen page – I can think of no verbal description of it. Six out of the next seven corrections are now accounted for; I have been obliged to skip one, which is of a different character, and will go back to it now.

When a fresh paragraph has been started at the wrong place, a curly line should be drawn, as shown, connecting the beginning of the new paragraph with the end of the last one, and 'run on' should be written in the margin. On the other hand, if the writer wants to introduce a new paragraph at some point where the printed text runs on, he should put a square bracket at that point and write 'n.p.' in the margin.

A wavy line beneath a word is an indication that it should be printed in black type, and 'bold' (the printer's name for black type) should be written in the margin. The word 'Capitals', which is so marked in the specimen page, also needs to be indented, i.e. slightly set back from the main margin. This is indicated by placing round the word a kind of semicircle, broken off at the point where the word should begin, and writing 'indent' in the margin.

It is not at all uncommon for a piece of metal, used for spacing, to get pushed up so as to obtrude itself in the letterpress. If so, put a line through it and make the appropriate conventional sign, an inverted T, in the margin. This is shown in the third line from the bottom of the specimen page; and the correction that immediately follows it shows the method of dealing with a broken letter – one arm of the 'w' in 'answer' has been chipped off. A circle round the faulty letter and a cross in the margin are all that is needed.

The last correction of all shows what should be done when you have inadvertently crossed out the wrong word in the text, or when you change your mind and decide that something which you had deleted should after all be retained. A line of dots should be made under the word or words deleted, and 'stet' (= 'let it stand') should be written in the margin.

It is not possible within a reasonable compass to deal with every contingency that may arise in proof-correcting, but I think that the illustrations given should cover the normal needs of most people. As it is, I almost feel that I owe some apology to the printers of this book for having coerced them into producing a page of type so butchered to make a proof-corrector's field day.

would think twice before writing 'Ex President' but many are quite prepared to write 'Nice Chancellor'; yet both are in exactly the same footing and in both the hyphen is equally essential.

I now have dealt with all the stops except the Apostrophe, which I mention merely in order that it may not feel neglected. It seems hardly necessary to state that it precedes the 's' of the possessive case in singular words (and plurals that do not end in 's') and follows it in plurals that end in 's' ('at his mother's knee', 'The Women's Institute', 'the Mothers' Union'); that to denote the possessive of singular words that already end in 's' it may either stand alone after that 's' or precede an extra one (St Thomas' or St Thomas's) and that with the possessive pronouns 'hers', 'yours', 'theirs', and 'its' it drops out altogether.

Having said that much (and I had almost forgotten to mention that it is also used to indicate the omission of a letter ('don't' for 'do not' etc.) – I feel that I have done my duty by the apostrophe. Would that all stops gave so little trouble! The remaining sections of this chapter, though not concerned with actual stops, seem to me to fit in better here than anywhere else.

Capitals. – I have often heard people say 'I wish someone would tell me the rules about the use of capital letters'. My answer would be, 'There are no rules – or at all events precious few – about the use of capital letters.

would think twice before writing 'Ex Presi-dent', but many are quite prepared to write 'Vice Chancellor'; yet both are on exactly the same footing and in both the hyphen is equally essential.

I have now dealt with all the stops except the APOSTROPHE, which I mention merely in order that it may not feel neglected. It seems hardly necessary to state that it precedes the 's' of the possessive case in singular words (and plurals that do not end in 's') and follows it in plurals that end in 's' ('at his mother's knee', 'The Women's Institute', 'The Mothers' Union'); that to denote the possessive of singular words that already end in 's' it may *either* stand alone after that 's' *or* precede an extra one (St Thomas' or St Thomas's); and that with the possessive pro-nouns 'hers', 'yours', 'theirs', and 'its' it drops out altogether. Having said that much – and I had almost forgotten to mention that it is also used to indicate the omission of a letter ('don't' for 'do not' etc.) – I feel that I have done my duty by the apostrophe. Would that all stops gave so little trouble!

The remaining sections of this chapter, though not concerned with actual stops, seem to me to fit in better here than any-where else.

Capitals. – I have often heard people say 'I wish someone would tell me the rules about the use of capital letters'. My answer would be, 'There are no rules – or at all events precious few – about the use of capital letters.

7

LATE EXTRA

THIS chapter is intended as a summary appendix to all the preceding ones (except that on Proof-Correction), in so far as they have not quite covered all the latest 'form'. English style, like most other things, is subject to changing fashions, which, even when they are hardly more than mannerisms, compel some notice. Punctuation is one of the handmaids of style, menial perhaps, yet capable of helping a mannerism to attract or to irritate. In their supporting role stops may play up to either the hero or the villain, as may be seen, for instance, from the following figure of speech, in vogue nowadays chiefly in fiction:

(i) 'There is no point in discussing it.' She put down the receiver.

(ii) 'I'll stand – I often do.' She got into the compartment before he could prevent her. 'I'll be all right.' The whistle blew. 'Look after yourself,' he said.

(iii) 'I'm not complaining,' – she raised her chin a little – 'I think I'm very lucky.'

(iv) 'I'm sorry.' She descended from the taxi. 'Which way do I go?' 'Why, down here, then straight on.' He gave a laugh at her ignorance, and she laughed too.

These sentences, as punctuated, are comparatively

inoffensive. The latest mannerism, however, is to punctuate as for an ordinary verb of 'saying' when in fact such verb is omitted, or is replaced by another of a totally different category. Thus the above, in their original form, appeared as:

(i) 'There is no point in discussing it,' she put down the receiver.

(ii) 'I'll stand – I often do,' she got into the compartment before he could prevent her. 'I'll be all right,' the whistle blew. 'Look after yourself,' he said.

(iii) 'I'm not complaining,' she raised her chin a little, 'I think I'm very lucky.'

(iv) 'I'm sorry,' she descended from the taxi, 'Which way do I go?' 'Why, down here, then straight on,' he gave a laugh at her ignorance and she laughed, too.

It is obvious that the punctuation is here the culprit, though the writers were presumably satisfied with the resulting absurdities, as must surely have been the author of this final instance, which, in part, defies stop-correction:

'I'm practically a native,' the manager smiled. 'I,' glared Bob, 'am a native.'

Since I remarked (p. 76) on the incorrect use of the QUESTION MARK where questions are reported, thus ceasing to be *direct questions*, I have noticed that this misuse is spreading not merely widely but also upward. Thus in a recent *Times* parliamentary report:

Z asked the Minister of Housing and Local Government whether he was aware of the continued shortage of housing in the northern region? How did this compare with that of other regions?

The first question mark should of course be a full-stop. The second, however, can stand; it closes what we may call a *semi-indirect* (or *semi-direct*, if you prefer) *question*, and I ought to have qualified my earlier remarks by mentioning that such do require question marks. There is also another form of *semi-indirect* that admits of them:

You ask me, how can I prove this? [*or* . . . ask me: how . . .]

But transpose two words only and the question becomes purely indirect – in fact a statement (needing no middle stop, moreover):

You ask me how I can prove this.

Again, in referring on p. 76 to what may be statements in form but are questions in effect, I might have mentioned also the converse:

It is a lovely day, isn't it.

Don't repeat that, will you.

Though both have the form of questions, the first of these is in fact a statement, the second a request – almost a command; and the writer will give his meaning more cogency by not using a question mark. For many pseudo-questions of this type, indeed, the exclamation mark is more appropriate even than the full-stop: e.g.

How dare you say a thing like that!

Recent fashions prompt a postscript also on INVERTED COMMAS. On the 'single v. double quotes' issue, usage in respect of quotation (or title) within quotation as shown on p. 80 holds good. There is, however, a tendency today to employ the two kinds for marking further distinctions, such as what may be termed *direct thought* (single quotes) in contrast with *direct speech* (double):

Thinking, 'This may be my last chance', he raised a forefinger and said, "I'll bid seventy-five."

This is often helpful to the reader. Single quotes for single words or short phrases in contrast to double for sentences is a fairly common habit, but less serviceable; whilst the practice, occasionally to be met with, of attempting to distinguish by this means quotations of the written word from those of the spoken word strikes me as merely tiresome hair-splitting.

Against the modern trend in some influential quarters towards banishing double inverted commas altogether I see two objections. Firstly, quotations are harder to pick out on the printed page when in single quotes – occasionally an important consideration. Secondly, and more important, the closing single quote often invites confusion with the apostrophe, as in:

It was reported that 'at the insurgents' request' negotiations had begun.

On the whole it seems to be wiser anyway to stick to one kind, whether double or single, throughout any one piece of writing than to ring the changes between them for the sake of distinctions that too often merely perplex or confuse.

Some of the less desirable ultra-modern figures of

speech could be, but usually are not, rendered a little less grotesque by recourse to the HYPHEN. For a noun to do duty as an adjective has long been legitimate and is often commendable, especially when the corresponding adjective would be clumsier than the noun ('maritime power', for 'sea power', for example). But nowadays, even where the reverse applies, it seems that noun must invariably be preferred to adjective. So instead of 'good materials' we must apparently have 'quality materials' (though quality may be bad no less than good); and the next stage ought at least to be 'high-quality materials', but more often than not the hyphen is absent and the phrase made all the uglier. And what about the further stages? – for there seems to be no limit now to the string of assorted epithets, whether noun or adjective, with which a single noun may be burdened. Look at these, for instance:

(i) A new tuberculosis attested herds scheme will come into force shortly.

(ii) He would miss his precious duty free pipe tobacco.

(iii) Those long suffering public nannies who run lost property offices have a hard life.

(iv) . . . long distance large seating capacity coaches . . .

(v) A hundred odd white cattle and sheepmen . . .

Not very elegant at best, these would at least look tidier, and convey their meaning sooner, as:

(i) A new tuberculosis-attested herds scheme . . .

(ii) . . . his precious duty-free pipe tobacco [*perhaps even* pipe-tobacco].

(iii) ... long-suffering public nannies ... lost-property offices ...

(iv) ... long-distance large-seating-capacity coaches ...

(v) A hundred-odd white cattle- and sheepmen ...

A common fault in somewhat similar instances is to stop short of the required number of hyphens. Thus 'her three-year old baby', 'a four-and-a-half mile long by-pass', 'the anti-fox hunting campaign', should obviously be 'her three-year-old baby', 'a four-and-a-half-mile-long by-pass', 'the anti-fox-hunting campaign'.

In general, writers, editors, and proof-readers need to be more alive to the *double entendre* that may result from omission of a hyphen. Here are some 'quick ones' to add to those given on p. 83 (note incidentally the special mischief-making propensities of the participle):

a sick berth attendant; a long standing member of the Assembly; two swarthy skinned foreigners; dope peddling rings; sport loving crowds; gum bearing trees; an officer producing organization [*à propos* the Cadet Force]; otter hunting enthusiast; egg laying hens.

All these, I may add, have exceptionally good references.

I feel less complacent about CAPITALS than when I originally wrote pp. 84-6, chiefly because of the present tendency to treat them as though they are slightly indelicate, or else extremely expensive. The habit of docking titles of their proper quota of capitals, noted in respect of *The Cambridge History of English Literature*, is spreading, and the result is, in my view, inconvenient for reference, unsightly in appearance, illogical, and often inconsistent. Why, for instance, refer in the same paragraph (as a leading newspaper lately did) to 'the Middle East ... south-east Asia ... North Africa ... south-west Africa'? Why (ibid.) always 'West Indies' but never 'West Germany'? Why 'Civil Service' but 'Civil servant'? Why 'the Master of Trinity' but (usually) 'the headmaster of Eton'?

Again, the normal treatment of words that have a special as well as a general meaning – 'state', 'power', 'government', 'allies', and the like – strikes me as anomalous. The usual practice is, even in the special sense, to capitalize (e.g.) 'the State' only in reference to our own, but to print 'a foreign state', 'European states', 'a state function' etc. In the interest of quick comprehension as well as of logic it is surely better to use a capital for the special meaning *always*, whether 'a' or 'the', singular or plural, noun or adjective, leaving lower case for the general meaning *always* ('he was in a critical state' etc.). Similarly, not only 'the Government' but also 'friendly Governments', 'a Government appointment' etc., as distinct from 'various forms of government', 'the reins of government', and the abstract sense in general. Indeed even where it is not a case of general v. special or abstract v. concrete – e.g. 'Minister', 'Ministry', 'Ministerial' in the political sense, 'minister' etc. in the ecclesiastical; 'Church' of the body, 'church' of the building – *meaning* rather than function (such as singular/plural, adjective/noun) gives the clearest and simplest dividing-line.

Finally here is a minor misuse of the capital that is becoming rather common:

We eventually effected a compromise: We would spend three days at Naples and a week on Capri.

The word immediately following a colon does not qualify for a capital unless it starts a quotation or *direct speech* – perhaps also *direct thought* (even without inverted commas): e.g.

He could not help reflecting: This time tomorrow I shall be more than a thousand miles away.

In conclusion I must needs return to the most ubiquitous, elusive, and discretionary of all stops, the COMMA, to complete my survey of the latest tendencies. I become daily more conscious of the almost universal carelessness of its treatment with relatives, and daily more firmly convinced that this carelessness is an offence against good English. Indeed if anywhere in comma usage there is room for a law of the Medes and Persians, I would confer that status on its function in distinguishing *non-defining* from *defining* relative clauses. However, I will not labour the point by adding here to the examples already given on pp. 55–6.

Next, a similar, if slightly less prevalent, carelessness is apt to mar the bracket-effect of a pair of commas (noted on pp. 20–22): e.g.

(i) A cryptic, and on the face of it, a foolish remark.

(ii) By the confidence, and at the same time the modesty of his manner, he managed to impart an extraordinary sense of reassurance.

(iii) He is principally concerned with the moral, even the religious content, of poetry.

(iv) The labour problems in nationalized industries are dealt with, or the ultimate decisions are taken by, men who were formerly trade union leaders.

(v) It was no mean trick to navigate by calabash and stick chart two thirds of the way and, in some cases, all the way across the greatest ocean at its widest point.

(vi) He maintained that much, even most of what they had done, was mistaken.

(vii) Certainly the most original, and possibly the most important religious writer France has produced in this century.

In all the above instances (and I could quote dozens more) the sentence is dislocated by the misplacing, or omission, of commas, as can readily be seen:

(i) A cryptic and, on the face of it, a foolish remark.

(ii) By the confidence, and at the same time the modesty, of his manner he managed . . .
Or:
By the confidence and, at the same time, the modesty of his manner he managed . . .

(iii) . . . the moral, even the religious, content of poetry.

(iv) . . . are dealt with, or the ultimate decisions are taken, by men who . . .

(v) . . . two thirds of the way, and in some cases all the way, across . . .

(vi) . . . much, even most, of what they had done was mistaken.

(vii) . . . the most original, and possibly the most important, religious writer . . .

[Note that (vii), and perhaps also (ii), could do without any comma at all; but in both it must be two or none.]

In the realm of the 'discretionary comma' there are today two opposite tendencies that I should class as indiscretions: the one involves too few commas, the other too many. The former has been rather scrappily handled earlier (see, e.g., comments on ambiguity on pp. 49, 50–51, 58–9, 64, 67–8), so that some further illustration may be useful – and it can be found, in even the best circles, any day of the week. Thus:

(i) The Governor wore a dark grey suit and his hair, cut short and grizzled, stood up in Prussian fashion.

(ii) As time went on the shelf ice dwindled.

(iii) He walked to the window and peered at some risk through the broken pane.

(iv) A great deal of course could be omitted.

(v) The Chinese adore statistics and above all percentages.

(vi) As it was Father Time, facing firmly to the west, turned his back on a dismal scene unfit for real cricket.

I submit that, in order to avoid the smallest risk of the reader's being led even momentarily astray, commas are needed:

(i) after 'suit'; (ii) after 'on'; (iii) before and after 'at some risk'; (iv) before and after 'of course'; (v) before and after 'above all'; (vi) after 'was'.

Further, I would point out that it is *the context only* that calls for these commas; not one of them is in a position that demands a comma on principle.

The opposite indiscretion has been, I hope, adequately dealt with in Chapter 3 (pp. 57–60); though the habit of attaching superfluous commas to adverbs and adverbial phrases – and often in the process luring the comma away from where it would be really useful – is becoming such a menace that it cannot escape a final taunt as Punctuational Enemy No. 1. While sparing the reader further instances of this abusage in its most fatuous form, I will close with a brief extract from a very recent work of one of the very best of modern authors:

... semi-professional, because in his off-duty hours, he played the viola in the local Shakespeare Theatre orchestra on Lavender Hill, and also conducted an amateur orchestra which, at some national festival, had been warmly praised by Hans Richter who had shaken this modest English postal worker by the hand, and told him that he was an artist.

Here, I would humbly suggest, a slight rearrangement of commas, misplaced both 'adverbially' and 'relatively' in the original, would make its tiny contribution felt, to the advantage of both sense and rhythm:

... semi-professional, because in his off-duty hours he played the viola in the local Shakespeare Theatre orchestra on Lavender Hill, and also conducted an amateur orchestra which at some national festival had been warmly praised by Hans Richter, who had shaken this modest English postal worker by the hand and told him that he was an artist.

INDEX

The figures in black type denote the pages covered by the main sections dealing with the various items

MORE ABOUT PENGUINS
AND PELICANS

Penguinews, which appears every month, contains details of all the new books issued by Penguins as they are published. From time to time it is supplemented by *Penguins in Print*, which is a complete list of all books published by Penguins which are in print. (There are well over three thousand of these.)

A specimen copy of *Penguinews* will be sent to you free on request, and you can become a subscriber for the price of the postage. For a year's issues (including the complete lists) please send 25p if you live in the United Kingdom, or 50p if you live elsewhere. Just write to Dept EP, Penguin Books Ltd, Harmondsworth, Middlesex, enclosing a cheque or postal order, and your name will be added to the mailing list.

The Penguin English Dictionary is described overleaf.

Note: *Penguinews* and *Penguins in Print* are not available in the U.S.A. or Canada

A modern dictionary for every Penguin reader

THE PENGUIN ENGLISH DICTIONARY

Containing more than 45,000 main entries, from the most collo-
quial words to the most formal, *The Penguin English Dictionary*
has been specially prepared and written for Penguins by a team
led by Professor G. N. Garmonsway, Professor of English in the
University of London (King's College) and is the result of seven
years' work.

The emphasis in this new dictionary is on current usage and the
entries include many hundreds of post-war words and senses, in
addition to the established vocabulary in English. Definitions are
given in the most direct and simple form possible, and the dictionary introduces a new and immediately understandable system
for pronunciation, which is likely to be of the greatest use to
foreign students of English.

We believe *The Penguin English Dictionary* can justifiably claim
to be an unrivalled catalogue of English words as they are used
today in print and speech.